# Battlefield *to* Ball Field

"Louisville Slugger has a long history of helping U.S. troops in war, dating back to World War I. We've supported troops with baseball and/or softball equipment in every major U.S. military conflict since. That includes World War II, Korea, Vietnam, Desert Storm, and now the wars in Iraq and Afghanistan. Since 2003 Louisville Slugger has worked to send more than 14 tons of sports equipment to our nation's dedicated soldiers and sailors in war theatres.

"Louisville Slugger is humbled and honored to be the equipment sponsor of the Wounded Warrior Amputee Softball Team. We remember that very first phone call with David nearly three years ago when we told him in the blink of an eye that we would provide their softball equipment. Of course, he and the team have been here many times and we always look forward to their visits. The guys have truly become part of our family."

*Hillerich & Bradsby Co.*
*Louisville, Kentucky*

"Since the Washington Nationals started working with the Wounded Warrior Amputee Softball Team in 2011, we have been in constant awe of the pure athletic ability – and maybe even more so, the intense dedication and strength of character – demonstrated by the players. Their stories serve as a testament to the resiliency of our country's service members, and convey a powerful message that the road to recovery – no matter how long – can lead to a full and satisfying life for veterans and their families.

Because the Nationals are a highly visible organization, we knew we could provide the WWAST a platform for greater awareness, and we're proud to have been the first Major League Baseball team to host them on a big league field. We're honored to have helped get them off the ground, and we take great pride in seeing how much they've grown in a short amount of time. These extraordinary individuals have represented the curly W well over the years, and we consider them an extension of the Nationals family."

*Mark D. Lerner, Vice Chairman and Principal Owner,*
*on behalf of the Lerner Family and the*
*Washington Nationals Baseball Club*

**ÖSSUR** ®

"The Wounded Warrior Amputee Softball Team's motto is 'Life Without a Limb is Limitless.' At Össur, ours is 'Life without Limitations.' While our respective organizations do very different things, we stand united on this common ground. The fact that the WWAST uses the devices Össur makes to compete against—and more often than not, beat—able-bodied teams makes us proud. But the fact that the WWAST also transcends the gap separating able-bodied from "disabled," uniting people in the process, speaks to the broader and transformative effect this team has had on the United States. We are honored to sponsor the Wounded Warrior Amputee Softball Team."

*David McGill*
*Vice President, Legal & Reimbursement*
*Össur America, Inc.*

"The Wounded Warrior Amputee Softball Team are truly amazing and heroes. It was such an honor to host them and have them come to our hometown of Sulphur, LA. We are beyond grateful and in debt to them for all they have sacrificed. They are all so inspiring and have touched my life in a special way as servicemen and now seeing all they have overcome and continue to overcome on a daily basis."
– *Jennie Finch*

"The Wounded Warrior Amputee Softball Team came to the Police Softball.com World Series and instantly became the heroes of 1000 police officers. Police officers are a group that doesn't impress too easily but now we all have someone to look up to."
– *Del Pickney - PoliceSoftball.com*
*Veteran / Police Officer*

"Having the opportunity to be involved with the Wounded Warrior Amputee Softball Team has been a life changing experience for our athletes, coaches, and fans of Arizona Softball!"
– *Coach Mike Candrea, Head Softball Coach*
*The University of Arizona — 8 Time NCAA National Champion*

"Please don't call me a hero" was often heard from the players of the Wounded Warrior Amputee Softball Team on their recent stop in the Northwest Florida Emerald Coast. If you can't call them heroes then there isn't a single word that 'labels' them in what they do, how they give back and how humble they are. These guys have survived unconsciencable injuries and numerous surgeries only to return as dedicated, elite atheletes that perform at the highest level without signs of any restrictions what so ever. They truly inspire with their message 'Life Without a Limb is Limitless.' They have become role models for everyone who has had to suffer the loss of limb(s); especially children!"
– *C. Donald Bishop*
*CEO, InDyne, Inc.*

# Battlefield *to* Ball Field

By
## Steven Clarfield, Ph.D.

**Preface by**
Jennie Finch

**Foreword by**
Tom Eisiminger, Jr
*Lieutenant Colonel,
USA, Retired*

**Clear Vision Publishing, Inc.**
Manalapan, New Jersey

PUBLISHED BY CLEAR VISION PUBLISHING, INC.
301 HIGHWAY 9 SOUTH,
MANALAPAN, NEW JERSEY 07726

ISBN: 978-0-9758541-1-2

FRONT COVER PHOTO COURTESY OF CUSTOM APPAREL, INC./NATE BRY
BACK COVER PHOTO COURTESY OF CAPTURED MEMORIES/KIM BERRY

PRODUCED BY WWW.BOOKSPRINTEDHERE.COM
MANAHAWKIN PRINTING
PRINTED IN CANADA
★★★★★★★★★★★★

Volume discounts are available.
Please contact Bill Miller
908-510-8644

# TABLE OF CONTENTS

## Photo Credits

Many hours went into the selection of the photographs used in this book. The publisher thanks all involved. The book is better because of your efforts. In addition, the publisher wants to thank the following organizations and photographers who graciously granted permission to use their photographs:

•*Captured Memories/Kim Berry*
•*Custom Apparel, Inc./Nate Bry*
•*Deloitte for permssion to use the photograph of Presidnets Clinton & Bush on page 140*
•*Haymarket Joe Photography/Joe Cashwell*
•*Lisa Macias*
•*Major League Baseball*
•*Kathy Manley*
•*Missfauxtography/Melissa Bergmann*
•*Össur/James Cassimus*
•*REUTERS/Gary Cameron*
•*Pete Sintes*
•*Tampa Tribune*
•*US Marine Corps*
•*USA Softball*
•*Work2Snap Photography/Kathy Manley*
•*Vanguard Magazine/Robert Turtil*

*Every effort went into obtaining permission to use the photograph and to credit them correctly. Please accept our apologies for any inadvertent errors. They will be corrected in future printings.*

*To Robert Clarfield, Lawrence Pasdiora, and all the soldiers, Marines and veterans of foreign wars who have served, or continue to serve, our country with honor.*

*To Vivian Clarfield, Thelma Pasdiora, and the loved ones of all generations who "kept the home fires burning" as they awaited a safe return.*

*And to those who have given the ultimate sacrifice for their country—may they rest in peace.*

# PREFACE

## BY JENNIE FINCH

I am so honored to be able to show a small token of thanks and appreciation by writing the Preface to *Battlefield to Ball Field*. I had the opportunity to meet and play against the Wounded Warrior Amputee Softball Team (WWAST) with FCA Softball in Florida, January 2012. I have always had tremendous gratitude for our servicemen, women, and their families. I was in awe when I met these true heroes and watched them play the game I love, and the game they love. It was amazing to hear their stories and hear first-hand how our game of softball had saved them and given them "life" after being injured. There is so much I love about our game, and camaraderie is at the top. These guys have that in abundance. To see them triumph over their injuries, take the field together, and show such beautiful athleticism — it was amazing. I knew they were special; special to so many, special to me!

The men on the WWAST captured my heart the minute I saw them. They have sacrificed it all. They have so bravely fought for us. They had setbacks, but they saw past that. They lived through it, and now they know no limits. The game we love has given them hope and life, and now because of it they are able to give hope and life to so many others. I knew I wanted to help the world see them. I wanted to help them share this hope that they are able to bring, and give them a little something back for all they have given to us. They have sacrificed for our freedom because our freedom is not free.

It is my pleasure to know these athletes and support them. I was able to bring the WWAST to Southwest Louisiana. Our community rallied around them in a way I am so proud of. I still cannot leave my house without someone talking about our Wounded Warrior event. The WWAST has impacted my life in so many ways. They all have powerful messages. They all have been through so much. They have fought and continue to endure through their daily pain and struggles, fighting every day, and all for us. They have overcome so much and are a living example of the best our country has to offer. Softball was just a game to me, but WWAST has shown me it is way more than that. They truly are America's favorite team, and they show every day that what can be achieved with enough faith and heart is limitless.

*Jennie Finch-Daigle*

*David Van Sleet & Tom Eisiminger, Jr.*

# FOREWORD

BY TOM EISIMINGER, JR.
*Lieutenant Colonel, USA, Retired*

## WAR·RI·OR [ WAWR-EE-ER ]

1. FIGHTER: SOMEBODY WHO TAKES PART IN OR IS
   EXPERIENCED IN WARFARE
2. SOMEBODY IN CONFLICT: SOMEBODY WHO TAKES
   PART IN A STRUGGLE OR CONFLICT

**W**arrior. By its very definition, the word describes each and every member of the Wounded Warrior Amputee Softball Team perfectly. Each of them volunteered to join the military knowing full well that they would be placed in harm's way to defend our country and our way of life. Each of them took part in and is experienced in the art of warfare, many of them leaving limbs behind on a distant battlefield as a result.

Every member of the WWAST also "took part in a struggle" to rehabilitate themselves, gain back what was taken, and regain their athleticism in their "new normal."

I well remember the day that David Van Sleet told me about his vision of a softball team consisting of wounded warrior amputees. David was extremely passionate about the potential for the team and what it could bring not only to the players, but to small town America. He mentioned at that point that the intent was to show that "life without a limb is limitless."

In March 2011, I was fortunate enough to be able to attend the session that was the very first time these Warriors got together to become a team. The energy, excitement, and enthusiasm of all of the players was evident from the very beginning. Having spent more than two decades in the Army myself, I knew full well the camaraderie that exists between a group of soldiers as a result of their shared hardships. In the case of these particular Warriors, the shared hardships not only included their shared hardships on the field of battle, but also in physical therapy and prosthetics clinics in military treatment facilities across the country. It soon became evident that these Warriors were very much interested in sharing hardships on what Douglas MacArthur called the "fields of friendly strife."

> *On the fields of friendly strife are sown the seeds that on other days and other fields will bear the fruits of victory.*
> – General Douglas MacArthur

I was able to watch many of their first games at George Mason University, at Walter Reed National Military Medical Center, and at the U.S. Naval Academy, and watch them develop into a team. David Van Sleet's vision is a reality, and the group of Warriors is now very much a team, as you will learn in the coming pages of *Battlefield to Ball Field*.

This team goes to small town USA on most weekends of the year and impresses the great American public with their resiliency, athleticism, and spirit. People who watch them play leave looking at their own personal problems in a significantly different light. The WWAST helps them understand that they can overcome their problems with a little bit of struggle and perseverance—a bit of a Warrior spirit, if you will. These Warriors are the embodiment of what is right with our country. If you work hard at something, you can and will be successful. In short, they make people across the country proud to be Americans.

David Van Sleet's original vision has grown into something bigger than perhaps he even thought possible in the beginning. The team now raises awareness, through exhibition and celebrity softball games, of the sacrifices and resilience of our military and highlights their ability to rise above any challenge—"life without a limb is limitless." The goal is to show other amputees and the general population that these athlete Warriors, through extensive rehabilitation and training, are able to live out their desires and play the sport they love.

The success of the team now allows them to give back for the greater good of society. The team supports local veteran causes, provides amputee-related education, provides direct donations to veteran amputee rehabilitation, and supports medical research related to veteran amputation issues.

The WWAST provides educational events to assist those that are living life without a limb. Their premier educational event is a Kids' Camp where amputee children are given the opportunity to learn from the experiences of the team. Additionally, the team supports amputation education at local Veterans Affairs Medical Centers when appropriate.

Very recently, the WWAST donated medically related items meant to assist in amputation rehabilitation to the Walter Reed National Military Medical Center in Bethesda. These donations are likely to extend to other military medical facilities where military veteran amputees are found.

Additionally, the WWAST will support medically relevant research that advance the lives of those veterans who have suffered amputations. Later in this book, you will learn of heterotopic ossification, which is a medical malady where bone grows where it should not. In the case of two of the Warriors highlighted in later chapters, this bone growth occurred on the end of their amputated bone, resulting in the need for further surgeries and a slower rehabilitation.

This book is the story of the first year of the development of David Van Sleet's vision. I am proud to have been a part of the initial formation of his vision and even prouder of the Warriors highlighted within these pages.

Most of these players are the age of my own two children, one who himself is a veteran of Operation Iraqi Freedom. I would be proud to call any of them son.

*"I cannot conceive that God has granted any man a richer, fuller, more satisfying life than me, for it was spent in service with, and for, that finest product of our civilization – the American Soldier."*
– General Matthew Ridgeway

# Wounded Warrior Amputee Softball Team
## Battlefield to Ball Field

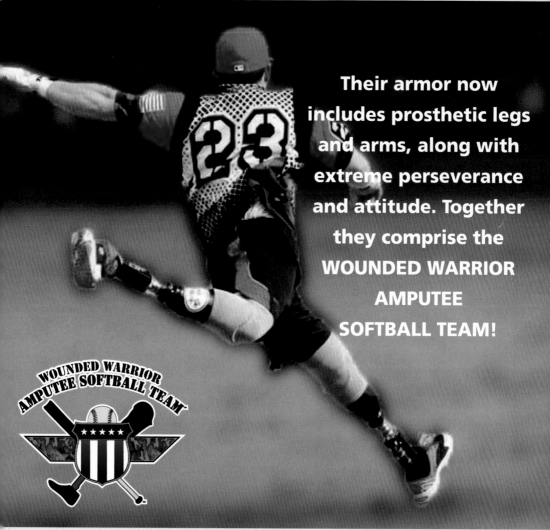

Their armor now includes prosthetic legs and arms, along with extreme perseverance and attitude. Together they comprise the WOUNDED WARRIOR AMPUTEE SOFTBALL TEAM!

PHOTO COURTESY OF LISA MACIAS

# THIS IS THEIR STORY!

# David Van Sleet
## Manager

# Matthew "Matt" Kinsey #12

Year Born: 1985
Hometown: Rockville, IN
Current Residence: Louisville, KY
US Army, Afghanistan
Amputation: Right Symes

# Joshua "Josh" Wege #23

Year Born: 1989
Hometown: Campbellsport, WI
Current Residence: Estero, FL
US Marines, Afghanistan
Amputations: Bilateral Below Knee

# Saul Bosquez, Jr. #30

Year Born: 1985
Hometown: Adrian, MI
Current Residence: Manchester, NH
US Army, Iraq
Amputation: Left Below Knee

# Nicholas "Nick" Clark #13

Year Born: 1981
Hometown: Yakima, WA
Current Residence: Puyallup, WA
US Army, Afghanistan
Amputation: Left Below Knee

# Timothy "Tim" Horton #34

Year Born: 1984
Hometown: Sulphur  Springs, TX
Current Residence: San Antonio, TX
US Marines, Iraq
Amputation: Left Below Knee

# Robert "Bobby" McCardle #8

Year Born: 1986
Hometown: Hales Corners, WI
Current Residence: Franklin, WI
US Marines, Iraq
Amputation: Right Below Knee

# Nathaniel "Nate" Lindsey #22

Year Born: 1985
Hometown: DeKalb, IL
Current Residence: Great Lakes, IL
US Army, Iraq
Amputation: Right Below Elbow

# William "Spanky" Gibson #15

Year Born: 1971
Hometown: Lawton, OK
Current Residence: Pryor, OK
US Marines, Iraq
Amputation: Left Above Knee

# Manuel "Manny" Del Rio #27

Year Born: 1986
Hometown: Van Nuys, CA
Current Residence: Martinez, CA
US Navy, Global War on Terrorism
Amputation: Right Below Knee

## Saul Bosquez, Jr.

# Nicholas "Nick" Clark

## Matthew "Matt" Kinsey

**Nick / Josh / Saul**

**Saul Bosquez**

# INTRODUCTION
## "DID YOU SEE WHAT I JUST SAW?"
## "DO YOU BELIEVE IT?"

My love affair with softball has taken me to hundreds of places throughout the country, as a player and as a spectator, to see remarkable events performed by outstanding male and female athletes. Yet, nothing in my 55 years on or near softball fields prepared me for what I experienced in August 2013 when I saw my first Wounded Warrior Amputee Softball Team (WWAST) ball game on an overcast, damp-to-the-bone afternoon in Panama City Beach, Florida.

Bill Miller—my softball traveling partner—and I had heard about this amazing team that did incredible things, and after a number of missed opportunities to see them closer to our homes in New Jersey, we decided it was time to trek the 1,200 miles to visit the guys at the United States Specialty Sports Association (USSSA) Military World Softball Tournament.

Imagine that you are unfamiliar with the Wounded Warrior Amputee Softball Team and are walking past a pretty ordinary softball field within a typical softball complex holding 12 fields in close proximity. At first glance, the scene is reminiscent of hundreds of other tournament weekends. As you look at the other fields, players of all shapes, sizes, ages, and ability are limbering up, taking batting practice, or just enjoying being in uniform and playing catch with teammates on a summer weekend. In the stands to your right, where a game has just begun, 500 or so spectators are cheering for the guys who have just taken the field. There's nothing unusual about that, you say, but then your eyes are drawn to the undeniable fact that each player on the field is missing at least part of an arm or a leg, and in some cases both legs.

The uniform neither hides nor camouflages what is missing. Nearly everyone has at least one prosthetic device that now functions as a replacement for a missing limb. Perhaps your initial reaction is to wonder whether you'll be seeing an exhibition of two handicapped teams working out near the able-bodied players. However, there are no prostheses visible on the batters coming up for the other team, and it's obvious they are ready to do battle. This is a game they want to win.

The game begins. The first batter hits a wicked shot past the diving third baseman, Saul Bosquez (Saul's action shot from another game is shown on the opposite page). Runner on first, no outs. The second batter hits a hard grounder to Saul again, who picks it up cleanly and throws to second baseman Tim Horton, who has a prosthetic leg, as Saul does. Tim tags second, for the first out, and while attempting to complete the double play, gets upended by a sliding runner, who carries Tim about 5 feet into center field. Bill and I looked at each other but didn't say a word. There was nothing to say except that there was a serious ball game being played out there.

Tim got up quickly. In fact, every member of the team gets up quickly. Every time they fall down or get knocked down, they spring right back up. The other player felt a bit awkward about taking Tim out and made the sportsmanlike gesture of shaking his hand once they were both on their feet, but I learned soon afterward that the only way you can insult this team is to not give them your best. Don't let up until the game is over, because Wounded Warrior Amputee Softball Team players approach every game like it might be their last and they wish to squeeze every ounce of competitive joy from the experience. Nothing is taken for granted, and their reason for being on that field is to re-experience what it means to be a ballplayer long after each had an experience that left him wondering if he would even live, let alone regain former athletic abilities.

The word "prejudice" has as its root the idea of pre-judging something without considering other possibilities. "Prejudice" describes how we think when we imagine what someone else should or should not be capable of because of some fact that we know about them. We think of these factors as "differences that make a difference," whether or not that is so. The most terrible part of prejudice is that it often provides a basis for feeling justified about excluding someone from experiencing something they might want to do, "for their own good." "We don't want them to get their hopes up and become devastated," is an oft-quoted bromide when trying to wrap a neat bow around a confusing and complex set of contradictions.

Until I watched my first Wounded Warrior Amputee Softball Team game, I never realized just how offhandedly prejudiced I had been when anticipating what I would be seeing and experiencing throughout the game. I didn't have experiences that put the word "amputee" in a context that sent a ballplayer head over teakettle while attempting a double play. That was reserved for able-bodied people who could take such punishment, or so my prejudicial ideas believed. Fairly quickly, that morphed into "Did you see that player move to his right and throw (off his prosthetic leg) from the hole to make that out?" "How does a man with two prosthetic legs hit a slow pitch softball over 350 feet?" "How did that man do so much after having gone through so much?" Until it became, much later, simply "That was a great play."

When I later spoke to David Van Sleet, whose ideas about

athletic possibilities of returning active duty soldiers, Marines and veterans was the primary impetus for bringing the Wounded Warrior Amputee Softball Team into being, he told me that my "Holy cow!" response to watching the guys go about the business of playing ball was typical. "By the second inning, the crowd forgets that they are watching amputees and sees two teams of ball players competing under even playing conditions. The crowd will even groan in the middle of a game when a player pops up with runners on base or fails to complete a great play, even while they can see that the player has one arm to make both the catch and the throw."

This game ended in a loss, and that provided this psychologist with an opportunity to observe firsthand how they handled this sort of setback. They didn't like it, but they tried their very best throughout the game and, as the cliché goes, "they left what they had that day on the field," which is all that anyone can ask. All encouragement for their teammates, good sportsmanship moments with today's opponents, and a promise that they would be better prepared for the next team they faced (whom they beat handily).

That day—or, more accurately, the next day, which brought torrential rains a day earlier than expected and enabled Bill and me to sit down with David to go over some ideas—was the start of a series of days, weeks, and months where I have had the privilege of working on a project about a team and a group of guys who, with stoic determination, incredible hard work, and a drive beyond anything I have experienced (certainly on a softball field) have pushed the competence envelope for themselves, those who have had the privilege to see them play and generations who will benefit from their example. The team's byword is "handicapable." Spend some time around them and it is easy to apply that idea to anything they set a mind to accomplish.

The title of this book, *Battlefield to Ball Field*, is the title that Phil Taylor, writing for *Sports Illustrated*, used in his July 4,

2011 back-page editorial on the team. It so captured the essence of where these men came from and how they approach games that David asked Phil for permission to use that title, which he graciously agreed to and we thankfully acknowledge. There have been a number of men and women who have contributed information found throughout this book with the same kind of generosity of spirit. The response we have gotten over and over again goes something like, "If you are a friend of the team, and they vouch for you, how then may I be of help?"

We are not attempting to make this book the definitive source for this ever-evolving team. Rather, we begin with a more modest set of goals. It is our plan to identify those therapeutic characteristics that have enabled the Wounded Warrior Amputee Softball Team to enhance the lives of their players, loved ones, spectators, and those who have seen or heard about them through national media. We will focus on the unique abilities of David Van Sleet to conceive the idea and turn the dream into a national treasure. His story is in the tradition of Branch Rickey's one-liner, "Luck is the residue of design," with surprising twists and turns along the way.

Each man profiled in this book is a military hero, although don't dare say that to his face. Real heroes don't like to be called that—it's just the way they are. To understand why this is so, you would have to explore ideas of patriotism, loyalty, commitment, responsibility and sacrifice, for starters. They each voluntarily joined up to fight for and defend their country, and hoped to spend a 20-year career in their selected military branch. And even after their traumatic injuries, if given the choice, they would be back at their post, supporting their buddies, protecting the home front, and serving their country.

## *The Wounded Warrior Amputee Softball Team*

The team name, consistent with the precision I've come to expect from David Van Sleet, tells its story eloquently in a few words. So let's examine that name. Each man on the team was wounded while on active duty and all of the infantrymen profiled in the book, four Army and four Marines, were wounded in either Iraq or Afghanistan while on patrol. The ninth member is a Navy veteran wounded on the flight deck of his aircraft carrier during takeoff maneuvers.

Each member of the team proved himself a highly trained and skilled warrior during his time serving in foreign wars, and then fought perhaps even more valiantly toward the goal of regaining what was taken from him by his injury. And when you see the way each one approaches the second-chance opportunities afforded to them on ball fields around the country, it becomes clear all over again that the label of "warrior" is an appropriate one. "Amputee" puts it right out there. Each of these men left a significant part of himself on some remote battlefield on what was otherwise a typical day of intense fighting in what had become the daily grind of doing one's duty while in harm's way. As you read the stories in each serviceman's profile, remember that the level of danger that accompanied their daily routine was fairly constant and the particular day in which the cause for amputation occurred was like most of the other days, except this time the bullet or the improvised explosive device (IED) didn't barely miss or bounce off some protective shielding, it got through to such an extent that each guy was down and fighting for his life a few moments after the shock of the assault. And that is also a fact of these men's lives. All of the guys who suffered IED injuries received wounds throughout their bodies, from head to foot, in addition to the inevitable concussion that is an all-too-frequent part of the list of traumatic injuries.

From the moment of injury, each guy became the responsibility of his fellow warriors, who took split-second action to shield their buddy from further danger and remove him from the battle, while stabilizing the wounds and applying tourniquets as quickly and skillfully as their sense of urgency and battlefield training would allow. In every situation that is described in this book, others, with or without injuries, selflessly did the right thing to save a life. And we know this because failure to stabilize the injuries that result in amputation would instead result in death within minutes.

All of the men on this team went through the physical, mental and emotional ordeal of becoming an amputee. And as they describe it, "it is what it is." So how is it that each man can play softball after losing so much? The answer is at the heart of this book's *raison d'etre* (reason for being). Go back to the color pictures that precede this section and look closely at each man back again on ball fields. The gap from traumatic injury to free-standing softball playing is more like a chasm and is certainly not bridged by the timid. It takes a combination of courage, talent, support, and good fortune for that transition to become possible.

Which brings us to "Team" as the final descriptor in The Wounded Warrior Amputee Softball Team. Teams, or at least those that prevail and make a difference in the lives of its members, are made up of people who value the benefit of being part of a whole that exceeds the sum of its parts. These are men who have had a lifetime of athletic ability and were able to turn their warrior spirit toward a dedication to get back between the chalk lines of a ball field from the moment they reached a bottom few of us can imagine. And that specialness was matched by David Van Sleet, a prosthetic professional and softball fanatic with the foresight and leadership qualities sufficient to turn the idea of amputees on a ball field playing exclusively against able-bodied opponents into a reality.

The Wounded Warrior Amputee Softball Team is now a traveling assemblage of active duty military and Veteran softball players who can be found most weekends stopping at a town or city nearly anywhere across the country, playing against a team whose skill level is a mystery. They have a win-loss record of something well over .500, but this overall statistic hides the facts that 1) as they get better known, the competition includes more and more ringers (ringers are talented players brought to a team to improve that team's chance of winning—the term is associated with both bragging rights and winning bets); 2) they have made it clear that they expect their opponents' best, no matter what the score; and 3) larger crowds tend to bring out the competitor in all of us—and even though I have heard opponents complain as they won games that "this is not the storybook ending," second thought tells them that this is exactly how the story book ends because the Wounded Warriors are not in it to win but to get a chance to be able to earn the win. Give them your best game and they are happy. The rest is up to them and that's just how they like it.

## *Research*

This is my third softball book. The first was about Ty Stofflet, my vote for the best fast-pitch softball pitcher and overall player who ever lived. It's entitled *Softball's Lefty Legend*. The second, *Best of the Best*, profiles the 19 top players and coaches in female fast-pitch softball over the past 50 years. Both of those books took the better part of a year to research and a season to write. For a psychologist with research training, it is important to cross-reference details and stay very close to the facts when documenting life histories. We ballplayers tend to have convenient memories and can be placed in one of two groups: those who embellish their accomplishments and those who would rather not dwell on them. Ty and the people profiled in *Best of the Best* were reluctant to spend time speaking about themselves, but were willing to make sure that the information described was accurate and thorough. When David read

*Best of the Best*, he found that his experience with the legends of the game mirrored what appeared in the book and wanted the same kind of approach for *Battlefield to Ball Field*. The biography of the team, it turns out, has a combination of adventure, mystery, and a parade of Prince Charmings and Fairy Godmothers that would make any fairytale proud, except that I have the corroboration and details to support a wild ride that both really happened and ends in the robust, healthy birth of a team.

The reluctance of the heroes in my first two books to speak about themselves provided a base for conducting the cross-country personal and phone interviews necessary to put *Battlefield to Ball Field* together. People wanted the story to be told, but did not want the focus to be on them, and so I remembered a fable about heaven and hell and worked out a plan. Picture a place where there is a table full of the most delicious foods anyone can imagine, that stretches out farther than the eye can see. People are sitting at that table without elbows and are therefore unable to feed themselves. They are starving. Now picture the same enormously extended, bountiful banquet in a different place. The basic structure is the same. Nobody has elbows, and yet everyone is enjoying their full share. Why? Because in heaven they have figured out ways to feed each other.

About 100 people have been interviewed in the course of researching the material for this book. Like the members of the Wounded Warrior Amputee Softball Team, they tend to tell their stories with a minimum of drama and hearts full of compassion. We have laughed together at awkward and painful moments that would be hard to understand without proper context. The guys themselves retain a stoic posture regarding their recitation, but there were many moments when family and friends had to pause for a time to wipe away a tear or regain the use of their voice. More than one hardened police or fire veteran has said that in a career that has seen more misery than they care to remember and generated more cynicism than they find healthy, the exploits of these veterans both on and off the field were sources of hope that have made a difference to their quality of life by providing (there's that word again) a level of inspiration that they thought had been drained out of them.

I, too, had heard it all, or so it seemed, within the confines of a therapist's office for forty years. I make it a practice to believe everything and nothing until I have enough information to establish some fact-based judgments. As far as I can gather and as deep as I went into life histories, each of these men is the genuine article—patriots who felt a calling to do their duty and who accept the hand they were each dealt without regret or recrimination. "It is what it is" becomes a first-step response to the question, "How do you begin a day at the height of your physical ability and end it forced to make decisions about how much of your body you are willing to lose to provide an optimal chance to survive and have a life?"

And once that has been established: "How do you decide to play ball on a team manned by fellow amputees against able-bodied opponents who have committed to play their best no matter what, in front of hundreds or sometimes thousands of people?" They are impossible not to root for and I count myself among the people who have learned a lot by their example after I thought I had seen it all.

## *What Makes the Wounded Warrior Team So Effective?*

What are the factors that have led to the Wounded Warrior Amputee Softball Team success? More importantly, can this be replicated by other community groups that are working to help veterans?

I believe the answers lie in the structure of the WWAST team, which employs one of the best models of cooperative support I have ever observed. For 35 years I have been organizing community organizations, sports teams, religious groups, families, schools, and private businesses into "teams" that employ the best practices of group cooperation in the pursuit of shared goals. My experience, which has been supported by a fair bit of research, is that individual members of highly effective teams demonstrate improved mental health as a result of their participation.

There is a difference, however, between healthy teams and unhealthy teams. When compared alongside dysfunctional groups, healthy teams excel in three primary areas. First, they care about each other. Second, they hold each other accountable by demanding that each team member perform at their highest possible level. And third, each team member is willing to sacrifice personal ambitions to support the goals of the team.

The first element, caring, is defined by how regularly each team member demonstrates appreciation, respect, and consideration for the other members of the group. This support can be time intensive, as evidenced by the countless hours that WWAST members have spent providing emotional support to other members of the community. But it can also be demonstrated in some of the lighter moments on the field. In 2010 a group of researchers at U.C. Berkeley found that NBA teams that demonstrated a higher volume of physically supportive gestures, such as pats on the back after a play, experienced higher levels of team performance. Healthy teams have teammates that care about each other, and we can measure this by the frequency, intensity, and quality of caring acts between teammates.

The second element, accountability, is a cultural measure of the expectations that team members have for each other. I have worked with many groups that have cared deeply for each other, but they will lose every athletic contest, business deal, or community project if they fail to demand a baseline level of performance from each team member. Maintaining both personal and group metrics for performance is an essential prerequisite for healthy, productive teams, and if teams fail to include this element, their members will lose many of the ancillary benefits that come with participation in a team that accomplishes something.

The third element, sacrifice, is measured by how willing each teammate is to set aside their personal desires when it serves the best interest of the team. In families it's the sibling that lets a brother or sister get credit from a parent, in businesses it's the employee that tackles an unglamorous part of a project because it helps the company, in sports teams it's the outfielder who plays second base that day because that's where the team needs a player. Healthy teams have to care and perform, but they also must cooperate.

The culture of the WWAST, as envisioned by David Van Sleet, is an embodiment of all three of these variables. Reciprocal caring among team members is evident in the emotional meetings with family members, the crowd of invested supporters, and the swell of high fives after both good and bad plays. Accountability among the players is easily observable in a group that gives each other no free passes on the field despite playing with amputated limbs. And sacrifice for the team, while a struggle for other groups, is just part of the code for a team of dedicated active duty military and veterans that have already given the highest sacrifice for their country.

The argument of this book is that, while the performance of this team may be unfathomable at first glance, it can be understood through the prism of these three factors. That is by no means to say that what this team has accomplished is easy. Caring, accountability, and sacrifice are an exceptionally challenging set of variables, and many talented, motivated, and otherwise effective people have tried and failed. This book is a testament to the adherence of the WWAST group to these three factors and a celebration of the success that has followed. Hopefully it may be a roadmap for other groups that want to follow in their footsteps.

# *Battlefield to Ball Field Structure*

The book is divided into two parts. First is a profiled biography of David Van Sleet—originator, coach, general manager, CEO, and organizer extraordinaire of the WWAST—followed by a history of the first nine months of team play, from March 2011 through November 2011. Consider this a heads up: If you ever consider trying to do something similar, David and the team's tale should give you pause. Rather than being anything easy to accomplish, it had fits and starts that generated serious doubts as to whether there could be such a team. With regard to the team chapter, more than 40 people who aided in the process of giving birth to this idea, program, and team concept told stories of what it was like to be part of something they believed in when its future was very much up in the air.

We are also quite fortunate to have a professional and personal description of the physcial factors involved in amputee movement, structure and function. Jessica Grede, DPT, has worked extensively with these athletes and is the older sister of Josh Wege. She has generously contributed to that description which is found in Chapter 3, at the beginning of Part Two.

The second part contains profiles of nine players who started with the team and agreed to be in the book. I am certain that their individual and collective contributions involved more cooperative and collaborative effort than anyone thought when they graciously agreed, but they kept their word and we are the beneficiary of their goodwill. We also had an opportunity to speak to loved ones and friends who went out of their way to be supportive and helpful. The Afterword describes lessons learned and what others must do if they wish to have similar successes for their projects.

Some readers enjoy going consecutively from the first page through the last. Others of you might want to go directly to the player profiles, which have been written as standalones.

The vision for WWAST athletes is one of pushing the limits of modern prosthetic technology with more and more applications. As founder David Van Sleet frequently states, "Our dream would be the return of our soldiers from harms way without the resulting loss of life and limb. Until such time, our vision is to support and honor our soldiers' and verterans' sacrifices, and to show other amputees and everyone who sees or hears about us that 'life without a limb is limitless.'"

There are three consistent themes that appear for each member of the WWAST. Each is an excellent athlete who experienced a measure of success in his youth and developed the foundation of a fierce competitor. That foundation was put to the test when each man faced the daunting requirements of recovery. In similar ways, they all found the ability to channel their competitive fire and fully focus on the business of healing. As they acquired experience with their new prosthetics, they exhausted all options until they could once again go out somewhere and beat somebody at some serious athletic event.

Each man also bought into the values of full-effort recovery by focusing on being the best that they could be while finding those whose level of seriousness could help push them to new standards. From the very beginning of their rehabilitation time (in either Walter Reed National Military Medical Center in Bethesda, Maryland; San Antonio Military Medical Center in San Antonio, Texas; or the Balboa Naval Medical Center in San Diego, California) they cared most about investing as much quality time as possible in getting better and better and better. This is a self-motivated group who pushed their personal best on a regular basis, and when they could, pushed others as well.

But most importantly, each of the men was strongly in the center of a healing community where they found people who could understand them, and in turn they passed what they learned to others. Whether helping or being helped, it has been a collective effort that allowed for no slack time and found continuous ways to be part of something bigger than themselves. Remember, each of these men were well-adjusted in their commitment to their military service and knew exactly how it was that they got hurt and what the progression of next steps necessary to overcome severely difficult odds would entail.

We begin with the story of David Van Sleet, a man who saw hundreds of returning injured servicemen and pulled together the wherewithal to make a difference in everyone's lives—including ours.

# Part 1
## *The Wounded Warrior Amputee Softball Team*

*Chapter 1*

# DAVID VAN SLEET
# "DEDICATED & COMPASSIONATE"

D avid Van Sleet is a man of many distinct and separate talents who has combined these gifts with a lifetime of digging deeply into ways to improve the lives of others. He is very serious when it comes to his extensive and intensive responsibilities, but his approach to these responsibilities never comes across as boring, desultory, or ponderous. Rather, if you want to have fun, get close to David and hang around for the inevitable good times that punctuate all of his relationships. Talk to anyone who has known him, whether for a brief time or a life time, and the story is the same. Sigmund Freud said that the child is the father of the man, and in David Van Sleet (as well as the others profiled in *Battlefield to Ball Field*) it is possible to take a thread that begins early in life and track that thread through the trials and tribulations that occur in a full life.

David is the second child of Jack, a former Marine and mechanical engineer; and Polly, a credit union manager with a certification in real estate. Both by reputation and my personal experience, Polly is an outstanding cook and hostess with a penchant for bringing friends and family together in congenial gatherings. Born and raised in Vermont, the Van Sleets have the erect bearing of the classic New Englander as they enjoy their retired life in Bonita Springs, FL in the midst of as many friends as one could imagine. I emphasize this fact because Jack and Polly's friendships played a critical role in the formative days of the team and even up to the present.

As I said above, David is Jack and Polly's second child, surrounded through youth by an older brother, Michael, and two younger sisters, Kim and Jody. The Van Sleets credit the closeness among the children as they grew up to the fact that this was a household where the parents got involved in their children's activities and a place where friends and relatives enjoyed gathering. Add to that Jack's availability and interest in coaching and Polly's commitment to keeping their social lives active and healthy, and opportunities for conviviality abounded. There is also a certain level of consideration and kindness from Polly to which my wife, Patricia, and I can attest. When Polly found out that we would be visiting the Southwest Florida Gulf Coast area to spend research time working with David on the book, she made sure to set places for us at her Christmas brunch table. For her it was nothing special, but for us it was a demonstration of the Van Sleets going out of their way for people they have never met on a very special family holiday—that is just the way they are.

In order to properly document David's talents, which have gone hand in hand with the inception and coming into being of the Wounded Warrior Amputee Softball Team (WWAST) let's start with early childhood. For proof of David's ability to make and keep friends, you can talk to several whom he has kept up with since elementary school in Burlington, VT. I have been with him on numerous occasions when he seamlessly managed a barrage of telephone and text communications with interest, good humor, and consistent respect, and that's not to mention the daily slate of emails that cross his desk. He has time to listen and complete each communication in a manner that is helpful and moves each process forward—but at the same time, he knows exactly how to let the other person know what he is ready and willing to do and what won't be happening. Clinicians understand that you never really accept a "yes" from a person unless you have had experience hearing at least one "no." As the saying goes, you can take David's yes's and no's to the bank.

David is predictable and precise. In a background conversation with Polly and Jack they made it clear that their children understood that they could try anything they had a mind to as long as they were willing to be accountable for their actions and could accept responsibility for any and all results. They also had as a critical part of their parental core value that it was not their job to micromanage what David and the others did. He was clearly a guy who was compassionate and considerate of others— how he made his way in the world was going to be up to him, so he might as well get used to those conditions early in life.

Almost everybody interviewed for this chapter was quick to identify that David's focus is on how he might be beneficial to someone else. In the tradition of other accomplished people mentioned earlier, he finds it a waste of time to place attention on himself, and requires a very good reason to engage in such a conversation (and discourages others from doing so). Left to his own devices, this would have been a set of storylines exclusively about the guys—however, that would leave much of the story untold, including just how David came to be the team's founding architect.

According to long-time close friend John Limanek, "David was best at being able to recognize other guys' talents and play to their strengths. We played on the same league basketball team at the YMCA when we were in the 7th grade. We didn't have the greatest team, but David always came up with a plan for us. I remember one game that David must have scored 20 points, as every time he saw I got the defensive rebound he sprinted to the other end of the court as I heaved the ball down to him for the easy layup. David has always enjoyed athletics, and really admires good athletes. David was always a schemer. In a good way. I think it came from having a big brother that was a super macho athlete. David and I were little runts compared to his brother Mike and my older brother Jim, who were also best friends. When the two big brothers were around, we knew it was best to stick with our own friends and make our own fun. David and I have taken very different routes over the years, but we've always remained close friends. David makes a real effort to get old friends together whenever he can. He cares a lot about his friends and always speaks so highly of them. He has made it to most of our Rice Memorial High School reunions even though he only spent the first two years there. When he comes back to Burlington to visit his family, he always makes sure to plan a gathering of friends too. When we get back together, it hardly seems like we've been apart. David is always so comfortable and fun to be with. He always has great stories of what he and his friends and family have been up to, and is genuinely interested in what has been going on in my life."

David has a passion for sports and organizing fun team events. He also has always shown a deep competitive streak that made second-best or failure particularly hard to take. In 8th grade, he decided that it was a good idea to put together a basketball team for a YMCA tournament. He sized up his Catholic Youth Organization (CYO) basketball team's chances and came to the conclusion that decisive action was needed to improve their championship potential. And so he reached out to better players from other CYO teams that he played against and assembled a team that put together a good showing throughout the tournament. You won't find it surprising that he lists a number of those add-on guys as good friends right to this day.

When Jack Van Sleet took advantage of a better "IBM" job

Photo courtesy of Haymarket Joe Photography/ Joe Cashwell

opportunity in Virginia, he moved the family when David was about to be a high school junior. The surface fact is that a guy from Burlington, VT was displaced to a school with 2,000 students below the Mason-Dixon line. It's not exactly a Yankee in King Arthur's Court, but he could easily be forgiven if he was the kind of guy to bemoan his new circumstances. As one of the team's slogans goes, "It is what it is." But that is not the way David thinks, feels, or behaves. Barry Hickey, one of his longstanding Virginia high school friends, remembers that it took almost no time at all for David to recreate the socially positive atmosphere that he had to leave behind in Vermont. He tells a story of David organizing an ice skating party for his friends that introduced skating to Virginians who did not have that activity on their childhood to-do list. Barry was also quick to point out that David was an accomplished skater and that it was an interesting way for the New Englander to establish his athletic credentials.

At the conclusion of his senior year, David was voted "Best

Personality" in the Fairfax High School senior class. So much for having to take a while to get accustomed to the new ways of his classmates. Instead, he is a consistently interesting and caring person who values inclusion and provides consistent examples of the fact that wherever David may be, shared and good natured fun can break out at any time. And don't put any of this under the heading of goody-two-shoes. This is a group that can dish it out as well as they can take it. Take yourself too seriously and you just won't fit in. Jim Rodio, husband of Susan Rodio, the WWAST Kids Camp Director, and life long high school best friend from Fairfax, Virginia who became Chief Financial Officer and legal counsel for the Wounded Warrior Amputee Softball Team, mentioned several moments when David, on his own, organized parties and sports events that seemed to invariably lead to good times. He was so good at it and did it so well that there was often no need for the others to do anything but make sure they got to the event ready to have fun.

He and his friends graduated in 1973, when the Vietnam War was drawing to a close. Having had parents who believed in self-reliance and wanting to serve his country before he settled in for the inevitable stint in college, David enlisted in the U.S. Army in the beginning of July 1973, just after he turned 18 on June 29th. "All through high school, the Vietnam War was going on. The war was ending. I wanted to serve my country and experience the military life. The Army offered a two-year enlistment program and I signed up." When Jack was asked how he felt about his son volunteering to go to war, he answered with a straight face, "I thought he was a fool…he should have joined the Marines [where I served]." Those readers who recognize each veteran's pride and loyalty to his or her branch of service know that Jack was telling it like it is.

David's idea was to get into the infantry and get a chance to be in the fight. "I had the time of my life in basic training at Fort Knox, Kentucky. It was all about exercising, running, firing machine guns, and throwing grenades." The best plans, however, can go asunder. David took a military aptitude test prior to basic training and scored so well that he was assigned to train to become a Nuclear Weapon Electronics Specialist at Redstone Arsenal in Huntsville, Alabama. "I was put in a class of 6 individuals, all of whom had higher education." They attended class and trained for seven months.

When he completed that program, he was assigned to Camp Ames near Chang Dong Ni, South Korea for a 12-month stint. And here is where we encounter another core characteristic of David Van Sleet—he is on the lookout to seize interesting opportunities, no matter how farfetched and remote they might seem to others. The work detail at Camp Ames provided a lot of time for soldiers to be on their own. David used that time in two specific ways: first, he became a prolific letter-writer in the age before email and instant messaging, keeping friends and family abreast of his activities while maintaining connection to those he cared most about, and secondly he decided it was time to become a basketball gym-rat.

Here we have a guy who is about 5' 7" tall, maybe 160 lbs, with a piqued interest but no particularly noteworthy abilities in basketball beyond general sports aptitude and sports smarts. He hadn't played high school basketball, and it wasn't even his first sport. But the gym was open and available and there were many unfilled hours that could be invested in this new venture. He made a quick assessment of his talents such as they were, and concluded that his best opportunity to become a member of a team worth joining would be to capitalize on his speed, quickness (they are different attributes) and court savvy (the ability to sense where the ball would be going) to get out on a fast break before his opponents could get under way to stop him. He also spent many hours learning to control the basketball as point guard, see the play before it occurred, and get the ball in the hands of his fellow players when they were open and had a high-percentage shot to take. And as everyone who has played or watched the position of point guard learns, this is a "pass first, shoot second" position unless you are out there on the fast break with a chance for the back-breaking easy layup, which is demoralizing to the other team not willing to hustle the way you are.

There is a saying in sports: "The ball always finds the guy who is afraid to catch it." The corollary is that diligent practice and focused attention to detail when tested on the court pays off handsomely. So in David's words, "Here are guys who played college and high school ball spending time at pick-up games in the gym. First I discover that I can play my position in pick-up games and later become the starting point guard on our military league team. That team became good enough to win the base championship."

His next deployment took him back to the States at the Seneca Army Depot in Romulus, New York. David simply says that they had a "need for his specialty" without clarifying what that statement means. But he was willing to talk about the Company softball team and Company basketball team that he organized. Here is the pattern that keeps repeating: he finds himself in a situation and very privately and personally makes an assessment about the gap between what currently exists and what might be possible with a combination of vision, top-level communication skills, and on-the-fly improvisation. Organizing and project managing are second nature to him, so once the worthwhile idea takes mental shape, he already has some sense of just what needs to occur for it to come into being. Some people are great at conceiving ideas. Others enjoy taking the blueprints and building a solid structure. David imagines the proposed structure, creates the blueprints, and starts gathering the people and building blocks together so it can happen. And there is one additional requirement: Life is too uncertain and far too short, so we all better make sure there is time to have fun and enjoy the journey.

He received his honorable discharge from the Army with a

Photo courtesy of Pete Sintes

*Ben Baltz & David Van Sleet*

rank of Specialist E-4. And about the same time he applied to George Mason University located in Fairfax, Virginia. "It was ironic," David said about his move back to Virginia. "Just as I move to Virginia, my father is offered another promotional position with IBM and my parents move back to Vermont." David attended his freshman year in college on the G.I. Bill and pursued an Education curriculum. And at the same time, it almost goes without saying, he got the guys together to form a softball team out of their local watering hole, T.T. Reynolds. According to both Jim Rodio and Barry Hickey, David arranged the logistics of the softball experience, including typed itinerary, and managed to get T.T. Reynolds to sponsor the team in leagues and local, regional and state tournaments. "We played a 100-game schedule, all over the state," said Jim, "and David took care of every detail." In a combination of appreciation and admiration, he continues, "All the rest of us had to do was be there ready to play where and when the schedule told us."

During his productive freshman year, David was doing a bit of soul-searching regarding his educational future. He wanted a more creative technology, and found his next educational stop matriculating on the G.I. Bill at Northern Virginia Community College, where he received an Associates Degree in Dental Technology and Liberal Arts. When asked about that interest, David noted that he and his dad shared an interest in visual aesthetics and working with their hands. The Dental Program provided opportunities to use these skills. But sometime during his undergraduate career, he attended a lecture on maxillofacial prosthetics, and as the saying goes, a light bulb went on in his head. "I was wide-eyed. I could be dealing directly with the patient. It changed my life."

At the completion of the lecture, David made a beeline to the presenter and asked questions as to how, where, and when he could enroll in this kind of program. He was told of an intense and rigorous two-year program through the Veteran's Administration (VA) in conjunction with Temple University that offered the curriculum. As David vividly remembers, "The VA Maxillofacial Prosthetics Program had a two-year prerequisite of a degree in dental technology. They selected one person per year for the program, and I was the one selected." The gleam in his eye as he recounts this moment of professional discovery flashes brightly to this day. He had found his calling, and he knew it.

*David Van Sleet & Josh Wege*

He was enrolled in the VA Maxillofacial Program in Wilmington, Delaware, headed up by Dr. James Schweiger and William "Bill" Burger. He graduated in two years with a Certificate in Maxillofacial Prosthetics, specializing in ocular prostheses.

"My task was to make sure the prosthetic eye matched precisely the other eye." Polly Van Sleet provides a bit of insight here about her son's choice of prosthetic specialty. "David has the eye and soul of an artist. He would spend whatever time it took to make sure that the prosthetic eye had the same coloring of the other eye. He is a perfectionist. He could do everything in his own office/laboratory to take the measurements, design, fabricate, fit and insert the eye, making sure the prosthesis was perfect. And, like his father, he is not a man to take shortcuts where quality is concerned." According to David, "I was fascinated with the medical, technical, and artistic components of my profession that would enable me to personally assist in recovery from disease and injury."

Once he graduated from the VA program he was employed on the West Coast for a brief time, but discovered that "everything I know, love, and do is on the East Coast," and so he worked a bit in the private sector before becoming Chief of the Prosthetic Restoration Clinic at the VA Hospital in Washington, D.C. Like other excellent practitioners who wish to gain a wider range of experience with more varied populations, David added a private practice where he was able to assist more non-veterans, women and children as a complement to the mostly male veteran population at the VA. It was here where he was able to work on patients who lost eyes from congenital conditions, injury and disease.

In 1991, David transferred to the White River Junction VT, VA Medical Center (VAMC), where he became Chief of the Prosthetic Service, which was an administrative position. But like most devoted clinicians he found that a year off making artificial eyes felt wrong, so he started an ocular prosthetics private practice in Vermont that served patients from Vermont, New Hampshire, and the Lake Champlain region of New York. Once a

Photo courtesy of Captured Memories/Kim Berry

clinician, always a clinician, especially when you have the skills, training, and sensitivity to experience what occurs when disfigurement is replaced by a new normal and life without the missing part becomes limitless.

Jack and Polly tell a story that you would never hear from David, but gets to the heart of his compassion. While working in one of the VA Hospitals, he passed a morose patient who stayed in his room because of disfiguring injuries to the face that caused others to cringe and made outside contact a source of emotional pain and suffering. David passed this fellow's hospital room daily, began to gain a bit of trust, and received permission from him to measure and fabricate a facial prosthesis for him. The veteran agreed, and on his own time, David designed a prosthesis mask that did the trick. The result was a veteran who could now with less self-consciousness make his way down the hallway to group rooms and recapture the social existence that had gotten away from him. The intervention was discrete, specific, and effective. Problem encountered, skill sets applied, problem solved. And I can assure you that that was one day in the life of a dedicated and quiet healer. I have seen other moments with similar levels of compassion, caring, and consideration, all delivered with effectiveness and efficiency in the absence of self-promotion or drama. In 1996, David Van Sleet was selected "VA Prosthetic Chief of the Year." In 2003 he transferred from his position at the White River Junction, VT VAMC to the VA New England Healthcare System Prosthetics Manager position. In 2006 he transferred from New England to become the VA Southwest Healthcare Prosthetics Manager.

It is while David was in the Southwest that he saw active-duty and medically retired amputees returning from the battlefields of Iraq and Afghanistan firsthand and started to actively think about how to expand athletic opportunities related to advances in medical care for the amputee, prosthetic improvements, and general knowledge about physical, mental, and emotional preparedness. Others interviewed described his eagerness to take the initiative to schedule sports outings and other field trips that were not a formal part of his job description—and with his organizational skills, these events were eagerly signed up for and enjoyed. What was turning in his mind was an expansion of the scope of possibilities for returning military personnel to meet unprecedented levels of self-sufficiency and competitive opportunity. He came to believe that the right group of amputees could stand on their own against able-bodied competition. They would have to have had a very high level of pre-morbid (before the amputation) athletic and team sportsmanship ability, a fearless disregard for public athletic embarrassment, and an unquenchable thirst to get back where they could once again play serious games against whomever showed up to play them. And, equally important, they had to want to be part of a team where the whole would be greater than the sum of the parts.

Before I move on to highlight moments in the team's conception and early history, I want to take the opportunity to get a little bit ahead of the chronology. The team concept and its originator and guiding force had an opportunity to be nationally recognized in a very special manner when David was nominated for and received the 2011 Department of Veteran's Affairs prestigious Olin E. Teague Award recognizing an employee within the VA whose achievements have been extraordinarily beneficial to the rehabilitation of war-injured veterans.

We'll begin with the article that John Bircher wrote, which follows immediately:

## *MOPH Salutes David Van Sleet Upon Receipt of the Olin E. Teague National Award*
### By John Bircher, MOPH Public Relations

The Military Order of the Purple Heart (MOPH) and the MOPH Service Foundation are proud to salute David Van Sleet, head coach of "The Wounded Warrior Amputee Softball Team" and a 30-year employee of the Department of Veterans Affairs. Van Sleet was selected as this year's recipient of the Olin E. Teague National Award for the creation and coaching of the Wounded Warrior Amputee Softball Team. The Olin E. Teague Award pays tribute and gives high recognition to the VA Employee whose achievement has been extraordinarily beneficial to the rehabilitation of war-injured Veterans. The ceremony took place on Capitol Hill on November 2, 2011 in the Committee Room of the House Committee of Veterans Affairs.

*Photo courtesy of David Van Sleet*

*David Van Sleet*

*Photo courtesy of Haymarket Joe Photography/ Joe Cashwell*

*MOPHSF President
Jim Blaylock
throws out
first pitch.*

This prestigious award is named in honor of former Committee Chairman Olin E. Teague who was considered Congress' most ardent Veteran's champion, authoring more Veteran's legislation than any congressman before him. He joined the Army in 1940 as a Lieutenant and participated in the D-Day invasion of Normandy. Congressman Teague was a highly decorated combat veteran of World War II, receiving two Silver Star Medals, the Bronze Star, and two Purple Hearts. While in Congress, he was also instrumental in improving benefits for servicemen's survivors. In 1956, he helped overhaul the survivor's benefits, with the creation of the Dependency and Indemnity Compensation (DIC).

Photo courtesy of Captured Memories/Kim Berry

In 2010, David Van Sleet saw a need for returning Veterans to get involved in their community and proposed the creation of an amputee softball team. With the direction, funding and grant obtained by the University of Arizona, Van Sleet was able to assemble a contingent of war injured amputees for the disabled sports team. Twenty Vets were brought in from around the country and The Wounded Warrior Amputee Softball Team was born. Twice a month, the team comes together to play able-bodied sports teams ranging from firefighters to military academy cadets, and police officers to the FBI (a team they easily trounced). And, to show their capabilities, they never play other amputees. After sustaining life-altering injuries, these young men had to rebuild and heal, doing so with the help of rehabilitation and prosthetics. They accepted their new physiques and relearned how to do many of the things they love, including softball. Although it has been a difficult path to the ballpark for many of the players, their determination and spirit shines through and can easily be seen over the course of a weekend when they usually play two games, oftentimes winning. The MOPHSF is a proud sponsor of the Wounded Warrior Amputee Softball Team.

# Chapter 2

# Wounded Warrior Amputee Softball Team
## The Idea Becomes a Dream
## The Dream Becomes a Team
## The Team Becomes a National Treasure

Towards the end of David's tenure with the Department of Veterans Affairs, the VA had put together a successful set of Senior-Level Federal Acquisition Certification for Program and Project Managers Training Courses that would require participants to identify specific actions that would improve and/or enhance the performance of their programs or projects to improve how we serve our Nations Veterans. This process, which required David to turn his project management success into a comprehensive design, was something everyone soon discovered he was ideally suited for.

David began his efforts by attending the weeks long Program/Project Management Training designed by the VA Acquisition Academy and the VA Learning University overseen by Richard Garrison, the VA Chancellor for Program Management School and administered by Learning Tree International led by

Brian Green, a Learning Tree Internet Consultant. The goal for this initiative was to assess the impact of VA FAC-P/PM training and to identify and implement needed improvements.

As part of the contract terms, Learning Tree had to review the Action Plans and report back to VA and VAAA on the progress of improving project management accountability. While most were very tactical — improving the Work Breakdown Structure (WBS), formalizing the Risk Register, or mitigating schedule variances — one Action Plan stood out beyond the pack: that of David Van Sleet.

When Brian first read David's Action Plan, immediately Brian knew he found someone special, who not only took his work seriously, but took the mission of the VA seriously. David took the unique perspective to not only improve his project, but as Abraham Lincoln stated — to improve the 'care for him who shall have borne the battle and for his widow, and his orphan.' David was inspired by this moment to improve his contributions to the VA and created an Action Plan like no other.

According to Brian, "We reached out to David immediately to determine how we could support this very special initiative, and we did just that. Anywhere and everywhere that an opportunity presented itself to draw attention to David and his "project," we took the initiative. But very quickly, David's initiative become its own self-generating engine, and all we had to do at that point was get out of its way.

"I'm honored to call David a friend, but I'm more honored to have been associated with this movement of shining a light on veteran causes, and getting to experience the positive impact that David's efforts have had on his team of wounded warriors. David is a hero; and I can't wait to see what he and his team accomplish next. This attention is well-deserved — for all veterans associated with this rehabilitation project — on time, on budget and definitely within scope!"

That project outline was used in conjunction with the grant

obtained by the University of Arizona Disability Resource Center (DRC) under the direction of Amanda Kraus, Ph.D., assisted by David Herr Cardillo, Assistant Athletic Director at the DRC and Janet Olson, Program Coordinator, to host and hold a Disabled Veterans Sports Camp. The first two successful week long camps the University of Arizona Disability Resource Center held were wheelchair oriented with David assisting the DRC in obtaining a number of disabled veterans to attend and conducting a Veterans Benefits Class. It was when the 2nd year camp ended that the Disability Resource Center decided to move the 3rd year camp to a cooler temperature month and when the University of Arizona students were in session. It was then David came up with an idea he proposed to the Disability Resource Center leaders that they consider hosting and funding the third year week long camp as a Disabled Veterans Stand Up Softball Camp. Once the proposal was accepted and approved, David's immediate challenge was searching for active duty soldiers, Marines and Veterans to attend the March 2011 University of Arizona Disabled Veterans Sports Camp held on the Tucson, AZ Campus. Utilizing his network of VA connections, and spreading the word and personally meeting as many people as he could, David developed a list of a couple of hundred candidates that he eventually whittled down to 20 individuals per the Disability Resource Center requirement.

Now that he had his chosen group, David did not want to burden the Disability Resource Center or the Department of Veterans Affairs for further funding but he knew he had to outfit and equip the participants beyond the first two camps. The first step was inaugurated when David's life long friend Jola Janczewski, Ph.D. and her best friend, David's sister Kim Billingsley, put together a fundraising event that raised $4,000. Next came equipment, which David secured through a generous donation from Louisville Slugger. The company, which has a lengthy history of supporting military causes dating back to World War I, invited David and a couple of his players to their Louisville, KY headquarters to pick out all of the equipment they needed. The participants were provided with the top-of-line composite softball bats, fielding gloves, bat bags and batting gloves personalized so that each player would have their own. As Rick Redman, Vice President of Corporate Communications for Louisville Slugger recounted it, the company wanted to make sure that "each guy got his own stuff—there would be no need to share with anyone during camp—and that each guy would be taking their own equipment with them wherever they were next playing softball." This thoughtful, personalized gesture from the leading baseball/softball sports equipment manufacturer in the country was exactly the nudge the team needed to survive its infancy. This support, which supplemented the grant money provided through the University of Arizona, provided David with the equipment and resources to put a trial version of the team on the field. David knew that once people saw this team on the field, and the players experienced the camaraderie, there would be no turning back.

## *Disabled Veterans Sports Camp – Walter Reed Military Medical Center*

Prior to camp, there were three guys—Matt Kinsey, Josh Wege and Saul Bosquez—who seized upon the idea of playing ball as a way to put a bit of extra-special focus on their workouts. Matt and Josh immediately decided that someone would have to demonstrate leadership in this quasi-military group, and there was no reason it couldn't be them as long as they worked for the honor. Since both were recovering at Walter Reed, Matt went home to Indiana to get his truck so they could practice the "new normal" ball skills to be the best there was at camp. They weren't aware of Saul, and Saul wasn't aware of them, but each man had that sensation deep in their gut that if someone was going to be the best, why not them?

Matt and Josh practiced throughout winter, indoors and outdoors, to put some experience under their belt. Their friendship demanded that Josh's bilateral below-the-knee amputee status not give him any breaks and that Matt would just have to learn how to throw and hit with power off a foot which was missing. But most of all they focused on the five tools of a solid player—hit, hit with power, field, throw, and run. Later, when one of Matt's great throws from deep in the shortstop hole made it to ESPN, he could recall all that it took to find the ways to make that play time after time.

In another part of the country, Saul Bosquez was viewing his rehabilitation as a personal challenge to regain the skills he needed to compete against the top players at camp. He knew that David had set a bar of top-flight competition, and he knew that the keys to leadership began with showing up ready to play. He was not going to show up to camp unprepared.

Matt, Josh, and Saul joined 17 other athletes on the University of Arizona campus in 2011. Athletes sense athleticism in others, and in interviews with the players it's clear that they instinctively understood which players were prepared to play. The serious ones, like Matt, Josh, and Saul, set the tone for the team by listening to coaching, working on improvement drills, and making it their business to become a member of a team that, although temporary, was of critical importance to their sense of well-being. Other players seemed initially more interested in the opportunity for a not-too-serious experience with the guys.

As the players came to understand quickly, this week was anything but a vacation. David was using camp to gauge the level of play independent of the opponent. 20 guys were split into two teams so that he could make a determination as to whether the idea of "free-standing" amputee softball worked as well as he had hoped it would. In other words, this was a test of current performance against required performance, but it was also a test of current performance against potential improvement. For that to be fairly tested, David would need ballplayers willing to hustle, compete, and help throughout the five-day period of the camp's grant.

One of those players was Randall Rugg, and he had an experience early in camp that helped define what the team would become. Randall is a right-handed batter with a right leg amputation, which means that his left leg is his lead leg while hitting. During camp, Randall turned on a ball and broke his "good" leg, also below the knee. The sequence that follows, confirmed by at least three sources, set the tone for the rest of camp. First, all the players, coaches, and trainers made a circle around Randall, observing the military code that no one is ever left behind. Another player with a different amputation then lightened the mood by joking, "I probably shouldn't be saying this under the circumstances, but if you had my condition you wouldn't be in your condition," which turned into a chorus of relieved gasps and laughter. Randall's leg was broken, but he would be okay. And without knowing him for long, the team immediately cared about him.

The camp was faced with a new problem, however, because the group of 20 is now 19. So what does David do?

Prior to camp, David asked Tucson VA Medical Center Prosthetist Alan Cota, CPO, to recommend a young man who could come to camp and watch this unique group of players take the field. Jake Thompson, 14, was selected, and he showed up at the opening of camp with his parents, Laura and Kurt. The goal, at least for David, was to see if the team could really have an empowering impact on the communities it played in.

Jake was born with a condition that required an amputation of his left leg before he could walk. For 12 of his 14 years, he was only familiar with moving with the help of various prostheses. Despite these challenges, however, Jake became the starting third baseman on his freshman high school baseball team.

David made the outside-the-box decision to replace Randall with Jake and see how the team handled it. Jake's first at-bat, under the watchful eyes of his new and encouraging friends, was a homerun over the outfield fence. At that point, even David began to believe that something about this team might be very special.

According to Jake, "It was an amazing experience, because I had never been around so many people that had worn prosthetics like me—and another amazing part of it was that they all seemed new to their prosthetic device, whereas I had 12 years wearing one. Since I was the one with 12 years' experience, I don't know any different way of moving, so I'm comfortable with it and I can run full speed with it. It was just very inspirational to see guys who have gone through so much … Here I was, having a whole new respect for these guys, watching them play after going through all they suffered."

Laura and Kurt added, "You know, as a parent, when you have a child who is born with an issue like Jake had, at first it's frustrating and you wonder how to function in life—and then you see him come to grips with the issue. We watched him go through Little League, and he was a very determined kid like everyone else, so throughout his entire life we've watched him overcome and inspire a lot of people. This is just another episode where we watched him bond with these guys on the field and knew that he already knew how to play. But the interaction with these guys was special. They walk with him. They talk to him. And every time we meet, they hug us. It's like we are a part of this very special family."

# *Training*

Once the camp participants arrived and took the field for the first time, David realized he had something special..., but a sense of community could only take the team so far. The team needed training, conditioning, and a baseline of skills. So he brought in three Assistant Coaches with various backgrounds in sports, softball and training to get the team in shape.

Taylor Billingsley, had this to say, "Before I got involved with the WWAST I had little experience with people who served in the military and no experience with amputees. Since meeting these individuals I am so honored to be involved in what they do. They have done so much for this country and continue to do so every day of their lives. They will always be an inspiration to myself and everyone else they touch."

Gary "Bucky" Weaver noted, "We all made a commitment to coach them like anybody else. We pushed them to be the best they could be. By the end of that special week in Tuscon, I realized the guys thought we were coaching them,when in fact they were coaching us. They inspire us all."

Kevin Farley, shared the following: "It was one of the most fulfilling experiences I'll ever have, a wonderful opportunity to give back to those who have given so much. The Wounded Warriors helped me more than they can imagine.

"Thank you all so much, hope I can do more in the future. Our nations kindness & generosity is always about those who serve, and never about it's government."

Mike Candrea, head coach of the 2004 and 2008 U.S. Women's Olympic Fast Pitch Softball teams, as well as the University of Arizona's head coach during 8 NCAA National Championship seasons, was on campus for the camp. In his words, Coach Candrea was "absolutely thrilled to have the opportunity to be on the same field with them, watching them go about playing the game with great energy, great excitement, and great enthusiasm. They never felt sorry for themselves, they just played

Photo courtesy of David Van Sleet

the game. When you watch them play, you are struck by their enthusiasm and willpower to be able to go out and pursue something that I'm sure they love doing. They never let their handicap become a handicap. I remember announcing them and people giving them standing ovations and flags being flown. It was just a great time to honor America and honor our heroes. I grew up in the Vietnam era, and you never heard much about anything. Now you have a chance to really put your arms around these guys and thank them and you can watch them have fun playing a game that we all love."

The camp week ended with a 10 against 10 game. At that game, it finally became clear to David that the training plan was working. The play was crisp, the players looked more confident, and the team looked competitive. David's original plan had worked. Now, it was time for everyone to take back the lessons they learned from camp and find the best local softball leagues they could.

Except there was a problem. The players liked each other. More than just liking each other, they felt a sense of community. When they were playing alongside one another, they competed harder, they pushed themselves further, and they demanded more from themselves. They wanted to keep this team intact.

David, however, had no funding and only the Louisville Slugger equipment to support what a team needed to continue. There was no league to join, no sponsors, and no fans. On the other hand, however, he had a dozen committed athletes, with a defined sense of purpose. They were fully invested in practicing, competing, and supporting each other. With that in place, could he find the other pieces to make this a real team?

## *A Full-Time Team*

David started by turning to his consistently supportive family, who once again rallied to his cause. Jack Van Sleet got together with friends Ed Eggly, Tom Callicot, Al Miotke, and Dave Stewart to form an ad hoc committee for fundraising and community service. Their first joint resolution was to put together an April 2011 golf tournament at their Highland Woods Golf & Country Club in Bonita Springs, FL to raise money for the team.

At the golfing fundraiser, a couple of the team members came to the golf club, did some meet and greets, told the tale of what could be, and demonstrated some substantial athletic skills. They received about $7,000 for their efforts, which gave David enough money to put together a playing weekend in the Washington, DC Metro Area and Annapolis, MD. His first stop was his old stomping grounds, George Mason University, followed by Walter Reed National Military Medical Center then a game against a U.S. Naval Academy team arranged by his sister Kim's good friend Maury Neiber.

At this point, the effort began to pick up steam. David began securing enough funding to bring the team to different locations. As the team visited new locations, they attracted new fans, enthusiasm, and funding. This turned into media attention, which brought new supporters to the team.

One of them was Robert "Bob" Duff, Chairman and CEO of FedComp, Inc. and the president of the Diamond Dream Foundation. Bob's work at the IT company had left him financially comfortable, and he was a lifelong baseball fan as well as a natural philanthropist. After hearing about the team and wondering if he could help, he invited David and two WWAST players to a Washington Nationals baseball game.

Before the game, Bob ran into Israel Negron, former Director, Community Relations and Marla Lerner Tannenbaum, the daughter of the owner of the Washington Nationals. This encounter was serendipitous, as Marla had previously heard about the WWAST and was interested in helping. Bob Duff took the initiative to introduce Marla and David, and then he got out of the way. To use his words, "I believe in karma. Do a good deed and it will come back to you. I made the contact because I felt David needed the help and the Nationals would be very interested."

Bob was also instrumental in helping set up the first game the WWAST ever played against an able-bodied team. This was also where Bob got his first full understanding of what the team was all about it. As Bob put it, "I thought, 'we're going to help these handicapped kids.' Once the game started, I didn't see one handicapped kid when we played them. They beat us 35 to 10 and then they let us get a few runs. It was a lopsided score. They were professionals. Professional soldiers. Professional in every way. They were each missing a body part, but it was more of an inconvenience than a handicap."

Bob played most of the same guys a year later. "When I first met the team at the hotel and then the next day, when they came out they were still in recovery. You could tell by the look on their faces. They were still struggling with the handicap. But the next time I saw them, they were just like the rest of their teammates. The transition of being on this team brought them back to finish the recovery. They were fine. They were relaxed and having a great time. They got back, mentally they got their limbs back."

This introductory series of games proved that there could be a competitive team, but it also affirmed that the team was going to need more funds to support the requirements of a group of guys who would need to travel hundreds, or even thousands, of miles to get to a weekend event. Bob Duff, through the Diamond Dream Foundation, presented the team with a $5,000 donation, which enabled the guys to go to Louisville, where the Louisville Slugger connection provided a free field and a number of amenities, including drivers to get the guys where they needed to be. But in order to make sure that the guys were properly treated, David had to put up an additional $5,000 to assure that there would be a trip to Louisville.

The increasing media coverage both helped and complicated matters. It started in Stars and Stripes and other military media, which gave the armed forces audience an introduction to David's nascent idea. The Washington Post followed with a Sunday feature by David Nakamura with pictures of the team. Rick Bozich wrote an article for the Louisville Courier-Journal that received national attention, and two days later Phil Taylor from Sports Illustrated made contact. Taylor's editorial, entitled "Battlefield to Ball Field," essentially described the WWAST as an American treasure.

For David, this exposure was confirmation that: 1) the idea works; 2) the dream is now a dedicated team; 3) you can play anywhere in the country because of your actual team coupled with your terrific organizational skills; and 4) the general expenses are a private fiscal burden of potentially massive proportions. To make matters even more complicated, Nick Dolin, Senior Producer for HBO Real Sports with Bryant Gumbel, had just reached out to David to film a segment with Frank Deford.

David responded by calling in a professional level of support. He asked his best friend, Jim Rodio, to help the team qualify for 501(c)(3) status, which meant that the WWAST would qualify for charitable contributions. Jim, a lawyer and supporter of the team, plowed through the red tape and got the 501(c)(3) status confirmed in record time. But there was still the underlying problem of funding.

At this point, David decided to go all-in. To date, he had been the founder, creator, head coach and promoter, but he finally became the underwriter, which he did in the form of $27,000 of his own money to the team. He gambled that if he could get a team of players ready to go back to Louisville and get a sufficient number to agree to participate in the interviews, the HBO segment could be the final spark that lifted the awareness of the team to a sustainable level. He would not be disappointed.

On the appointed day, with HBO assembled for the occasion, the WWAST went through its paces as though the guys had been doing it for years. The segment, which originally aired on July 19, 2011, was a hit. It showed a dedicated group of veterans regaining personal, professional, and athletic confidence in a unique setting, as only the WWAST could. Suddenly, the team was a national story.

In looking back on the piece, Nick, Frank, and the HBO team all agreed that they understood in the moment that they were capturing something special. According to Nick: "They were terrific. We have worked with lots of people, and obviously when you work with professional athletes it's a very different experience. These guys were very early in their experience with the WWAST and they were just beginning to get some attention for what they were doing … The most powerful thing to me about the story was that it was vitally important that they not leave their athletic lives behind as a result of their injuries and their amputations. And for all of them—and any athlete can understand this—they just wanted to play and they wanted to be part of a team."

Once the HBO story hit, the team was on fire. The next stop was a trip to Oklahoma City, where they played a team of military officers from Tinker Air Force Base followed by a split team game with the USA Men's Slow Pitch National Team. This resulted in an invitation to go to Panama City Beach, Fla., for the USSSA Military World Softball Tournament. At the USSSA Military World Softball Tournament, Jeff Jackson, VP of Business Development for DRASH, presented the team with a $25,000 donation. At their next tournament, in Danville, IL, they played in front of 5,000 fans, their largest crowd to date. From there, they traveled back to Washington, D.C., to play a game against a team of Washington-area celebrities on the Nationals' home field after a Washington Nationals game.

The team now had fans, funding, and competition. What started as David's dream of teaching and coaching wounded soldiers, Marines and Veterans had been forged into a tight unit of softball players barnstorming the United States. It was everything David could have imagined, and an undeniable product of his hard work, intuition, and moxie.

What David didn't understand at that time, however, was what this experience was beginning to do for the players, families, and communities. In his original thought process, he envisioned some of the byproducts of this success, but at the Camp stage there was no way to capture the impact this level of success would have on everyone. As the players in the following chapters demonstrate, the answer was bigger than anyone could have imagined.

# Part 2
# *The Players*

*Jessica Grede utilizing manual therapy to address pain and tightness in Nick Clark's forearm muscles.*

*Chapter 3*

# Preparing to Win

## *by Jessica Grede, DPT*

Take a moment to observe a few things about your-self. First, look at how you are holding this book. Are you using one hand, or two? Notice the grip you are using: how many fingers it requires and whether or not you use any part of your palm. The next time you tie a pair of shoes, think about the intricate movements and fine motor skills required to do so. Also, be mindful of the amount of motion at the knee, hip and lower back that allow you to reach your foot in the first place. What about the tasks of buttoning a shirt or zipping up a coat? If you have kids or grandkids, how often have you bent over to pick them up using both arms, stabilizing through your legs to maintain balance, without thinking twice about it? Negotiating a flight of stairs requires a fair amount of strength in the legs and hips, but if you have ever done so while wearing a ski boot, you can also appreciate the range of motion required at the ankle. Now try to imagine performing these tasks had you lost a couple of fingers, a hand, or a portion of your arm or leg.

The task of walking, or gait, may seem like an automatic, simple task, however for gait to be successful it requires the interaction between the neuromuscular (muscles of the body and the nerves that innervate them) and somatosensory systems. The somatosensory system, comprised of a number of receptors in communication with the brain, allows us to determine where our body is in space (proprioception), how our body is moving (kinesthesis), and identify harmful or painful stimuli through the sense of touch.

There are two distinct phases during gait, stance and swing. Stance phase begins with heel strike, or contact of the heel onto the ground. As the body moves forward onto the leg, weight bearing begins along the outside portion of the heel. Mobility at the ankle joints allow the foot to flatten out or roll towards the middle as the body passes over the foot and the heel lifts off the ground, shifting onto the ball of the foot. Muscles and other structures in the bottom of the foot, along with the calf muscles, provide force to propel the body forward. This phase, toe off, finishes rolling off of the big toe and the foot leaving the ground. Once the big toe leaves the ground, swing phase begins and muscles in front of the hip bring the leg forward. For the toes to clear the ground as the leg swings forward, muscles in the back of the thigh bend the knee while the shin muscle bends the ankle to pull the foot up. As the leg strides out in front of the body, muscles in the front of the thigh activate to straighten the knee and position the foot and ankle for heel strike. The arms swing to drive trunk and hip rotation, maintain a fluid motion and aid balance. This pattern is amplified when it comes to running. More power is required from all of the muscles to propel the body forward during toe off. With longer strides, the joints have to move through a larger range of motion which in turn requires greater lengthening and flexibility of the muscles.

Balance and proprioception play a large role in gait. Proprioceptors in the extremities give you feedback about how fast and how much your arms are swinging, whether or not your trunk is upright, where your leg is in space as it swings through the air, and what position your foot is in as it contacts the ground. It also gives you the necessary information needed to successfully balance on one leg for a brief period. If you have ever started to roll your ankle, you might have found yourself stumbling. You stumbled because your body was aware that tissues were stretching too far, too quickly. The somatosensory system made your brain aware that if this motion continued, the soft tissues would likely be stretched beyond their limits. The resulting action was therefore a stumble, or a very short stance time on the ankle that was rolling with a quick "hop" onto the opposite leg to avoid injury.

Every member of the Wounded Warriors Amputee Softball Team wears a prosthetic on at least one of their limbs, with the majority having suffered a below-the-knee amputation. This means that part of their somatosensory system, which is the system of receptors between your brain and limbs, is no longer available to aid balance and give feedback about foot position. Sensation stops where the residual limb ends, and beyond that is a prosthetic that needs to be maneuvered and controlled. Running backwards is difficult when you have no visual input about where the foot is landing behind you, and even more so when you cannot feel the foot at all. The lower leg and foot muscles, especially of the calf, are no longer available to help transition from a static position to a forward sprint or lateral shuffle.

The Wounded Warriors were forced to begin adjusting to these constraints the minute they returned home. It is an adjustment they never complained about, and it is the element of their story they prefer to dwell on the least. But to understand the will of this team, and to truly appreciate what they accomplish in every game, it helps to have a sense of what each player experiences on and off the field as a result of their injuries.

*Matt Kinsey* suffered a Syme's amputation of the right foot due to the extent of his injuries. A Syme's amputation is the complete removal of the foot, at the level of the ankle joint, along with the end of each of the lower leg bones. Although much of the tissue of his lower leg muscles remains, he lost the attachment site for them at the foot. Think of a pulley system—action on an object can only be produced if the string is attached at both ends; otherwise, the pulley itself is of no benefit. The lower leg muscles have atrophied to a large degree since his amputation, as they are no longer used to help him walk.

Matt has a long socket with a flexible carbon fiber foot-piece attached to the end of it. Unlike the rest of the team members that have a below-the-knee amputation, Matt has no pylon in his prosthetic. The benefit is that the extra length of his residual limb provides more balance and stability; however, he has very little to work with if adjustments for leg length are needed. Matt's right leg tends to be longer than his left due to the design of the prosthetic foot. This leg-length discrepancy alters the alignment at his hip girdle and lower back. In any case where there is an alteration in alignment, the mechanics of the joints and length of the soft tissues involved are directly affected. This often leads to pain, irritation, and possibly breakdown of tissues or structures over a long period of time. For Matt, inserts added to the shoe of his sound limb act to minimize his leg length discrepancy.

Matt plays shortstop for the team. He has to be ready to react quickly and cover more ground than a first or third baseman. Matt has to be able to turn and twist his body and maneuver his feet to run into the outfield for a short fly ball, make lateral strides to get behind a hard grounder, or aggressively charge a slow roller. Matt constantly pushes off of his prosthetic leg to generate force for a hard throw across the infield. To cover second base and turn a double play, he must first find second base with his prosthetic leg and then make a throw. Matt does not allow the limitations of his prosthetic to prevent him from playing softball as he had prior to injury. He continues to make diving plays, chase down balls that spectators might initially think are out of reach, and adapt to the changes between the sand of the infield and uneven ground of the outfield to do it.

Matt bats right-handed, making his prosthetic leg his back leg while at the plate. As he strides forward with the left leg, he is forced to balance on his prosthetic foot. He needs to maintain his balance and stabilize most of his body weight through the toe portion of his prosthetic foot as he pivots and forcefully rotates his hips and core to powerfully drive the ball. Next, he has to transition into a sprint to first base, usually by pushing off his prosthetic leg first.

**Bobby McCardle** suffered a below-the-knee amputation. Bobby's prosthetic of choice while he plays is a running leg or c-shaped blade. These prosthetics are incredibly functional and efficient for straight, forward running. The blade is made of carbon fiber, making it very strong yet pliable, which allows for a "springing" motion. The "spring" gives high energy return to propel the body forward in the absence of the foot, ankle joint and surrounding musculature. However, if you have ever looked closely at one of these, you may have realized there is no foot-piece attached at the end of it. Instead, the blade is only a few inches wide with what looks like the sole of a tennis shoe on the bottom of it. There is no heel, making it more difficult to decelerate and come to a stop after a sprint.

Despite losing his right leg below the knee, Bobby is a versatile member of the team, playing either first, second, or third base. As an infielder, he needs to be able to balance himself in the ready position and be agile enough to move in any direction to field the ball or cover a base. In Bobby's case, the design of the prosthetic aids his momentum while running and assists in giving him the agility needed to play the positions he does. His specific prosthetic has a longer toe lever, which increases the surface area in contact with the ground. This allows more energy to be stored throughout the carbon fiber blade as the prosthetic contacts the ground to simulate a more natural gait pattern during toe off. A longer toe lever works to equalize stance time between his sound limb and prosthetic to achieve a more fluid gait. Although there are definite functional benefits to the design of this prosthetic, a drawback, especially when it comes to playing softball, is the lack of a heel and ability to wear a shoe.

Bobby needs to rely more heavily on the heel of his left leg to come to a stop. Quick lateral movements to the right require a little more effort to stop and control. While receiving a throw at first base, Bobby needs to position himself with most of the weight on his left leg and prosthetic foot on the base. At times, he has to quickly adjust and move for a ball that may be less than a perfect throw. When at third, Bobby has to be able to transition and move in response to the hit. After he stoops to field a grounder, Bobby has to shift his weight onto his back leg and engage his core. In doing so, he must balance on his prosthetic and then generate a forward force to activate his hips, core, and shoulder girdle to make a hard throw across the infield.

While at bat, there is further need to balance on his prosthetic leg and also generate force and initiate the motion of the hips and core. The "spring" in his running leg aids his ability to sprint to first base after he hits. But, during the hit, Bobby needs to adjust for any up-and-down motion that may occur in his prosthetic. If his body rises and falls even slightly, it affects the plane in which he is swinging while trying to make contact with the ball. Bobby is still able to stabilize his lower body well and drive his arms through the ball for solid base hits.

*Manny Del Rio* lost his right leg below the knee. Manny shares many of the same challenges as Bobby, since they both wear the same type of running leg prosthesis on the right leg, although Manny has his own challenges to deal with given the position he plays. As a pitcher, Manny pushes off of his prosthetic leg with every pitch he throws. If he is off-balance at all, it results in the rest of his body, his arm especially, having to compensate.

Being off-balance may also affect the accuracy of the pitch. Once a pitch is thrown, Manny needs to quickly prepare himself to field the ball. Imagine Manny having to lean to his right to field a ground ball. He must lean over and maintain balance on his prosthetic to pick up the ball. Upon standing, he has to shift from the right to left leg as he turns his body and makes a throw. Since he is the closest to the batter, Manny has the least amount of time to react if a ball is driven back at him. Maintaining a stable base is important not only to play the game, but also for Manny's safety. If he is off-balance, it will be harder to quickly move out of the way or react to a line drive up the middle.

Like Bobby, Manny has to balance and dig in with his prosthetic to drive hip and core rotation when batting. Too much rocking and therefore shifting of weight from one foot to the other may increase up-and-down movement, thereby throwing off his visual field and affecting where contact is made with the ball. The more stable Manny can be in the batter's box, the better chance he has to create power through his body.

*Tim Horton* lost his left leg below the knee at the same time he received fractures to both elbows. The right arm, his throwing arm, required a metal plate. Although Tim has since regained full range of motion of each elbow, the elbow on his throwing arm does not fully function as it once had. An able-bodied person can increase reliance on the lower body for more force production and decrease stress at the shoulder and elbow in the event of an injury. In Tim's case, his plant leg when throwing is his prosthetic leg. Instead of using the lower body to assist the arm, he often has to demand more from his arm, given the limitations of his prosthetic. This increases Tim's risk for an overuse injury of the shoulder or elbow. Tim often battles soreness in the shoulder and elbow following a game, especially if he has done a lot of throwing.

Tim's prosthetic has a racing shock attached directly to the back of the pylon. The shock works to absorb force through the limb during heel strike. The amount of tension in the shock is adjustable to allow either a soft or more firm feel as the heel hits the ground, according to personal preference. The foot piece is composed of carbon fiber and allows for some spring to facilitate forward progression during toe off.

Tim is most often the second baseman, and he has many responsibilities. The majority of the ground between first and second is his to cover and take charge of on defense. He has to be able to turn either direction and run down a short fly ball that is out of reach of his fellow outfielders. At times you will see him backpedaling as he makes that final stretch to catch the ball and make an out. If there is a runner on first base, Tim has to be ready and able to do one of two things—after he sets himself in his ready position, he has to be able to immediately transition any direction and field a ground ball, or if the ball is hit on the opposite side of the infield, he has to push off of his prosthetic leg and sprint to second base. In order to turn a double play, Tim moves quickly and efficiently. A throw from second base is shorter in comparison to shortstop or third base, but speed and accuracy are still incredibly important to beat the runner. Tim has to plant and throw over his prosthetic leg. If he does not maintain balance or stability with his prosthetic, his accuracy is affected. This is what makes watching Tim turn a mechanically sound double play so inspiring.

When batting, Tim shares a common challenge with many others on the team. As a right-handed hitter, his prosthetic leg is his stride leg. As previously mentioned, this means a lack of proprioception as the leg lifts into the air, strides forward and plants down onto the ground. He too has to rely heavily on his prosthetic as he transitions from the batter's box to sprinting towards first base.

*Saul Bosquez* lost his left leg below the knee. He also lost a large portion of the big toe and smaller portions of the second and third toes on the right foot. During the phase of toe-off in walking and running, the last contact point to propel the body forward and generate force is the big toe. Saul has lost some of that lever arm on his right foot, besides having to overcome the challenges of having a below-the-knee amputation on the left leg.

Saul has not had any adaptations to his footwear to make up for what was lost on his right foot. Although the big toe is instrumental in gait and balance, he has been able to adapt and function extremely well while missing a large portion of it. The prosthetic he wears on his left leg has what looks like a small ball in the pylon. This component allows for some rotation through the prosthetic, to make up for what was lost at the ankle, and decrease rotary forces on the knee joint. A titanium coil spring helps absorb shock during heel strike. Like the other prosthetics discussed, his carbon fiber foot-piece is also flexible.

Saul has played first base, shortstop and outfield for the team but his primary position is third base. Prior to the ball being hit, Saul needs to balance his body weight through the ball of each foot and ready himself to sprint forward, or move laterally in either direction. If the ball is hit hard down the third base line, Saul will plant off of his prosthetic leg and dive to his right to make the play. Although the dive is impressive, think about what has to follow: As soon as the ball is hit, his able-bodied opponent is running to first base. If Saul makes a diving play, he has to first return to his feet, decreasing the amount of time available to make the throw across the infield and beat the runner. As a result, his throw needs to be even harder than normal, requiring him to shift his body weight and rotate his core through a greater range of motion with more power to assist his right arm. Imagine the effect this has on balance. Saul must first push through his incomplete right foot and throw his body weight over the left leg, but then immediately use his prosthetic to balance and counteract the forces that want to continue carrying his body forward.

When Saul is at bat and the pitch is coming in, he shifts

back and bears most of his weight through his right leg. As he prepares to swing, the left leg lifts and strides out in front of him. During the swing, his hind leg pivots on the ball of the foot and weight goes through the toes, part of which are missing, in order to generate force through the hip girdle and core. If he does not maintain balance and a stable base of support, it will greatly affect his swing and how hard he can hit the ball. Once the ball is hit, Saul has to again push off of the right foot and immediately transition onto the left leg to propel himself forward into a sprint with his prosthetic.

*Nick Clark* sustained a below-the-knee amputation on his left leg as well as injuries to both eardrums, and at times has some ringing in his ears. Thankfully, the injuries to his inner ear have not resulted in additional effects on his balance.

Nick plays left field and wears a modified running leg consisting of a blade with the addition of a foot piece. The benefits of the blade are the same as described for Bobby and Manny, with high energy absorption and therefore return when running. However, because there is a foot piece attached to the blade, Nick can wear a shoe and therefore gains more stability and control. As an outfielder, this becomes incredibly important as he sprints across uneven ground. The faster Nick can run down a ground ball, the less likely the runner is to gain another base and be in better scoring position. Nick is no stranger to sacrificing his body for the ball and has made countless diving catches to ensure an out. To field a hard grounder, Nick has to be ready to react and perform specific cutting motions at any given movement if the path of the ball is redirected by the uneven ground of the outfield. Once the ball is in hand, Nick needs to make the long, hard throw to the infield. He winds up and forcefully propels himself over his prosthetic leg, which in turn has to generate just as much force from the ground up to prevent his momentum from creating a fall forward.

Nick often bats lead-off for the team, placing added pressure on him to ensure a base hit and allow his teammates to drive him in for a run. Nick does well generating force with his right leg to swing, but his prosthetic leg must lift off the ground and stride forward. Nick has only so much ability to tell where that prosthetic is in space. An over-stride can be the difference between a hard-driven line drive or a pop-up to the infield. Once the ball is hit, it is his prosthetic leg that takes the first-step to initiate forward momentum into a sprint.

*Josh Wege* lost of both of his legs below the knee and fractured a vertebra in his lower back. Although his back has since healed, he continues to battle tightness and, at times, pain. This is contributed to by the history of injury directly to the spine, but also having to stabilize more through his core muscles than he had to prior to injury to his legs. The amputations resulted in the loss of a number of joints and muscle groups which make up the ankle strategy that our bodies use for feedback and balance. He has had to completely relearn where his center of mass is to maintain balance between both prosthetics. After he learned how to distribute his weight evenly in all directions and gain stability, he needed to learn how to maintain that during activity. As a result, he has to constantly engage his hip and core muscles more than he did prior to injury. To begin any type of movement, Josh has to shift his body weight to engage his prosthetics rather than simply push a foot into the ground to initiate movement.

Like Nick, Josh wears a modified running leg on both limbs consisting of a blade with the addition of a foot-piece. However, Josh does not have a sound limb to assist his injured leg and control movements. By attaching a foot onto the blade, Josh has been able to function much more efficiently and with less energy expenditure than he had with previous prosthetics. Each of his prosthetics is two to three pounds lighter than what he had been wearing. The high energy return of the blade aids his ability to run faster and even jump to a degree. Including a foot on the end of the blade increased the amount of surface area in contact with the ground. As a result, he has more stability, can utilize the heel to come to a stop after sprinting, and can perform cutting, change of direction, and lateral movements.

Despite missing both of his feet, Josh has played every position on the softball field for the Wounded Warrior Amputee Softball Team. He is most often seen pitching or playing first base. While getting ready to field a ball on defense, Josh bends mostly at the hips and only slightly at the knees. He leans his body weight forward and balances on the toes of his prosthetics so he can more easily move any direction to field the ball. As the first baseman, Josh is moving and involved in almost every play. He often has to take a couple of steps backwards and find the base with one of his prosthetic legs to then receive a throw from a fellow teammate and make the out. Countless times, Josh has been known to end up in the splits as he scoops a low thrown ball. Although this is a sight to see, what is far more impressive is his ability to jump and clear the base by a number of inches to grab a high throw out of the air. As most people do, Josh generates force through his hip and thigh muscles to accelerate his body upward. However, although his prosthetics can aid to a degree, he lacks the ankle joints and calf muscles to propel himself into the air.

In the batter's box, Josh has to first find a comfortable balance between each leg. As the ball comes in, he has to transfer his body weight to the right leg as he strides with the left, putting him in single-leg balance for a brief period. Josh pivots on his right leg and has to maintain his balance on both prosthetics while his hips and core rotate as the arms extend to hit the ball. Next, he has to quickly maneuver his feet and transition into a sprint to first base. When it comes to running, Josh has to rely on the sensation and feel through what is left of his limbs to obtain feedback about where his feet are in space and as they come in contact with the ground. And yet, you will see him crossing his feet as he moves laterally and twisting and turning his body while running. Whether he is batting, running, fielding or throwing a ball, he is constantly balancing between each prosthetic while his center of mass is being thrown in all directions. This is all happening in the absence of mobility in both ankles and in the muscles to control the ankles and lower limbs.

*Spanky Gibson's* injury occurred directly to the knee joint itself, forcing him to have an above-the-knee amputation. All of the same challenges of a below-the-knee amputation apply to Spanky; however, with a significantly shorter residual limb, he loses even more stability and function. The powerful quadriceps and hamstring muscles no longer aid Spanky as he negotiates stairs or stands up from a chair. The gluteal and other hip muscles pair with his core to facilitate movement and function in the absence of the majority of his left leg.

An above-the-knee prosthetic needs to be more complex than that of a person with a below-the-knee amputation. Control at the knee joint is instrumental in so many daily activities. When standing up from a chair, the gluteal and hamstring muscles work to extend the hip while the quadriceps straighten the knee. It is natural for a muscle to shorten as it contracts (concentric contraction). When sitting, those same muscle groups are at work but this time it is a more complex task. The muscles have to maintain a contraction but at the same time lengthen in a controlled manner (eccentric contraction) to support and lower your body weight rather than allow you to fall down onto the chair.

Spanky's prosthetic is designed to not only allow for knee range of motion, but also replicate the amount of force generated by the large quadricep and hamstring muscles. It is programmed with his specific height and weight, then uses that information to carry out an appropriate gait pattern. There are different modes to which the leg can be set to match the activity he is doing. The knee component of Spanky's prosthetic is equipped with a gyroscope, which is used to measure orientation, and monitor where the leg is in space, essentially working to replicate the somatosensory system that was lost. This same technology is utilized to rotate a picture on your cellphone as you turn your phone. Microprocessors in the knee work to sense different pressures and forces to then apply appropriate resistance for the task at hand. The foot piece of his prosthetic is similar to that of the rest of the team members in that the heel accepts force to soften heel strike and the foot itself is pliable to aid toe-off.

Spanky is involved in every pitch as the team's catcher. He constantly needs to stoop and bend to the ground to grab the ball after the pitch is thrown. He still has to make lateral movements or turn and run after a pop up behind the plate. When Spanky moves to his right, he has nothing but the left hip and gluteal muscles to push himself with. He does not have the option of incorporating additional lower leg and thigh muscles to create more power. For Spanky to make a throw, he keeps most of his weight on the back leg rather than transferring onto the prosthetic. This requires more core activation and torque on the shoulder since the lower body cannot assist as much, therefore increasing risk of an overuse injury.

At the plate, Spanky's mechanics in hitting need to be completely different than most. He bats right-handed, keeping nearly all of his weight on his sound limb. Spanky relies on his upper body to hit and generate force while his lower body is simply working to maintain balance. After he hits, Spanky runs to first base with his prosthetic leg set to a mode that allows for free swing. His entire prosthetic is brought forward by use of muscles along the front of his hip. The momentum generated by swinging the leg forward then snaps the knee into extension as he lands in heel strike. As functional as this prosthetic is, it will never allow Spanky to run as fast as he once had. There are times when the sensors don't get things exactly right or the timing is off.

*Nate Lindsey* shines a new perspective on the ability to function with an amputation as we now take a closer look at an upper-limb prosthetic. Nate lost his right arm, which is his dominant side, below the elbow. He no longer has the wrist mobility or fine motor movements of the fingers to rely on for daily tasks or self-cares. As a result, Nate had to relearn how to do everything with his non-dominant hand. Nate has overcome this to such a degree that by watching him, you may think he has always been left handed.

Nate's prosthetic consists of a liner on the residual limb followed by the socket. Unlike a lower-limb prosthetic, Nate wears a harness, rather than a second outer sleeve. The harness attaches to the socket and wraps up and around his upper back to then loop under his left shoulder. Because the harness needs to stay tight enough to firmly hold his prosthetic on, it limits mobility at the shoulder girdle. Think of the last time you wore a fitted dress shirt and tried reaching forward or up overhead for something. The lack of stretch or give in the shirt may have limited your range of motion such as the harness does in Nate's case. At the opposite end of Nate's socket is a hook that allows him to grip an object.

You will never see a better example of "finesse" than what Nate portrays in right field. Nate times his movements perfectly as he charges a ground ball, fielding it with the glove on his left hand. In a split second, you will see him with the ball in that same hand making a hard, smooth throw to his cut off. With one fluid motion, Nate scoops up the ball into his glove, flips it into the air, throws the glove off of his hand, and catches the ball midair to make the throw. He has reprogrammed his body and can now use almost flawless mechanics to throw with his left arm. Of course, this task entails much more than just the arm. He has had to shift gears and now steps with his right leg instead of his left. His body has to rotate in the complete opposite direction from the one it rotated in before to allow for a wind-up and then follow-through as the left arm comes over his body. To better appreciate what Nate has overcome, take a moment and challenge yourself with a throw using your non-dominant arm.

Nate bats right-handed, meaning his left hand is at the base of the handle with his prosthetic hand on top of that. Wrist mobility is key to having a powerful swing. Normally, both wrists bend slightly toward the thumb side as the hands begin to move toward the ball. Right at contact, the wrists bend down toward the little fingers and roll over. Nate has to rely only on his left arm for much of this, though he can still generate a wrist-roll with his right, as this motion occurs at the forearm. Sound swinging mechanics involve full extension through the elbows as the arms drive toward the ball. The manner in which Nate's prosthetic is fitted and attached to his limb does not allow full extension through his right elbow. However, Nate constantly overcomes these challenges in the batter's box to drive the ball for solid base hits.

Reading about the pain, suffering, and challenges may make many readers wonder why each player didn't elect to remain at home and reduce the possibility of sustaining further injuries. It also may raise the question of whether or not it is worth the struggle that each player endures just to participate in a recreational event. Considering the work it takes to regain the range of motion, strength and coordination necessary to complete normal day-to-day activity, isn't the challenge of high-speed fielding, pitching, and batting too ambitious?

As you will see in the next few chapters, each player has discovered that the physical costs are greatly outweighed by the mental benefits of actively engaging on the field with teammates. One of the greatest mistakes the therapeutic community can make is telling a person with physical constraints to taper their expectations for what they can accomplish. This turns the physical constraint into a mental constraint. By embracing the challenge of competitive softball, and engaging in cooperative team play, each player pushed back against the physical challenges outlined in this chapter and regained a mentally, emotionally, and athletically healthy life. That is the message at heart of this book, because it is the message at the heart of the team. As the team says, "Life without a limb is limitless."

*Jessica Grede grew up in Campbellsport, Wisconsin as the oldest of five children. During high school, She participated in volleyball, softball, and basketball and continued to play volleyball and softball at Carroll College (now Carroll University) in Waukesha, Wisconsin. Her passion for sports and interest in the anatomy and physiology of the human body paved the way for a career in physical therapy. While at Carroll College, she received a bachelor of science in 2004 with a major in psychology. She obtained her Doctorate in Physical Therapy from Carroll University in 2007.*

*Throughout her career, she has had the pleasure of working with a wide variety of patients including pediatrics, persons with brain and spinal cord injuries, and various other neurological and orthopedic conditions. In working with such a diverse population, she has developed a specific interest in treating and designing rehabilitation programs for athletes, pediatrics, and patients with amputations. Currently, she works in an outpatient orthopedic clinic based out of Fond du Lac, Wisconsin.*

*Dr. Grede's most recent career opportunity has been working with the Wounded Warrior Amputee Softball Team. First a fan and incredibly proud sister of Josh Wege, she now travels occasionally as the team Physical Therapist. While on trips, she works to manage any previous injuries, current complaints of pain, and most importantly, implement strategies for injury prevention.*

*Chapter 4*

# Matthew "Matt" Kinsey

## "Born to Play Ball"

On June 2nd, 2010, Matt Kinsey was on a night sweep patrol in a "hot" area of Afghanistan that had previously seen a large number of American casualties. While covering the rear door of a building so his platoon could exit, Matt stepped on an IED that exploded on impact. His right foot was amputated as a result.

A little over two years later, Matt went 3-for-3 in the 2012 MLB All-Star Legends Softball Game in Kansas City, Missouri. Of his three hits, one was a single that drove in Hall of Famer Andre Dawson, and the last was a home run. His National League team beat the American League 21-8, and at the end of the game he was named the Most Valuable Player.

Matt's amazing journey from hospital bed to MVP starts in Rockville, Indiana, where he was born in 1985 to Mark and Sherry Kinsey. Matt was born 8 years after his brother Mark Jr., an accomplished ballplayer and all-around athlete. Second-borns are often in a hurry to catch up with first-borns, and Matt was no different. He wanted to be part of everything that Mark Jr. did, whether that was playing catch in the backyard, watching him at football practice, or helping Mark Jr. train with their dad.

Matt's entire family was relentlessly supportive of his interest in sports, and as he grew older they encouraged him at every step. As Matt tells it, "When I was a little boy, I would be sitting at the end of the driveway waiting on Dad to get home to play catch. I had both our gloves and ball in my hand ready to go to play. Dad was always ready to drop whatever he was doing to play catch with me. Then when I got older, my mother allowed me to take batting practice. I bought wiffle balls and my mother would go out with me in the side yard and throw batting practice."

Matt's enthusiastic participation in sports caused some scheduling conflicts with the family, especially since his brother was so involved in athletics and his dad was the high school football coach. But, as Matt says, "We made it work. We still had family dinners every night, whether we got in at eight o'clock, nine o'clock, or whatever. We still all got to sit down and have dinner as a family. I know that was really cool."

In many ways, sports was the thing that really brought the family together. When asked about his mom, Matt said "She loves watching her boys play ball. She wanted two sons and she got her wish...she's like the ultimate sports mom. To this day, my parents come out and watch me play. Mom has always been that kind of mom. If I need an ice pack for a hurt body part, she brings it to me. I don't know how many times she has fed the football teams and baseball teams that have come to our house in high school or growing up. She was a sports mom. But then, of course, with Dad being a coach, that's just the lifestyle. I'm 28 years old and still playing ball, and they try to come down and watch me play as much as possible. And it is just so awesome to run out on the ball diamond and see your folks up there. To this day it's still cool. I'm sure...hopefully when I'm in my forties, still playing ball, they're still able to come watch me play. I think that would be great."

Rockville, Indiana was the perfect place for someone like Matt to grow up. His mother's side of the family worked in agriculture, so he split his time between farming and playing ball. When Matt and his brother came of age, Matt's dad decided to stop coaching the high school team and started coaching his son's travel teams, which gave Matt the experience of having an experienced high school coach, as well as a caring father, guiding his early athletic development.

Matt's 6' 3", 200-pound frame, natural agility, and cannon arm also helped. It made him the prototypical high school quarterback and earned him a starting pitcher/catcher role on the baseball team. The combination of his family's training and his natural athleticism made Matt a force to be reckoned with on whatever ball field he stepped on.

But high school was also Matt's first experience with adversity. During his sophomore year, he felt a tightening in his rotator cuff, and when he visited an orthopedic surgeon he was informed that he might never throw hard again. According to the doctor, "You can either play first or second, but you're never going to catch and you're never going to pitch again." Matt told him that he was wrong, but the doctor replied, "I don't see it happening. Good luck to you."

The response of both Matt and his family planted many of the seeds that help explain how someone can return from a battlefield foot amputation to All-Star MVP. Matt selected the path of rehabbing the shoulder, and he followed a plan that initially stopped him from throwing for three months. But he started lightly throwing a baseball in the off-season, and in the winter he worked on building up the shoulder in the weight room with his dad.

Next spring, the arm started feeling good, and Matt began throwing without pain. As he completed daily therapy and the arm felt better, he started throwing pitches at half strength. He also learned how to throw a slider in order to take some of the pressure off of his arm from his fastball, which had been topping out in the upper eighties (mph).

Finally, one day at practice, he decided to crank it up. He threw his traditional fastball over the heart of the plate, heard the pop of the glove, and knew he was back. He wasn't scheduled to pitch until the middle of the season, but after he showed his baseball coach his rehabilitated shoulder, the team put him on the mound the next night. The opponent was the No. 1-ranked team in the state.

Matt struck out thirteen batters on the way to earning a complete game victory. On the mound, he felt like his old self, with his fastball, curveball, and newly developed slider all clicking. When he got off the mound, he asked what he was hitting on the radar gun, the final determination of whether his arm was rehabilitated. For seven innings, Matt was back in the upper 80s. The doctor was wrong. And Matt still has the game ball to this day.

## Basic Training

At the end of high school, Matt received offers to play Division I baseball, but his efforts on the field didn't always translate to the classroom. As Matt recalls it, "I wasn't mature enough to handle it yet, so I went to a junior college, Danville Area Community College, to play baseball. I had a pretty good fall ball season, but being eighteen and away from home for the first time, I didn't handle it well. I really wasn't ready to go to college and my arm was acting up again. When I got back home from the spring semester I just didn't want to go back. I hit my limit. I didn't like school."

Matt started out on a friend of the family's farm, and his dad helped get him on the football coaching staff. He enjoyed the father-son time and gained a great deal of respect for what coaches do. And he was happy. As Matt says, "Here I was, coaching football with my dad and farming. It was a good life. I enjoyed it. I felt a passion for coaching."

But despite being content, Matt always felt a nagging itch

to join the military. Part of it was that one grandfather had served in the Army, one had served in the Navy, and his uncle was an active-duty paratrooper. But Matt also knew that the country was fighting a war in Afghanistan, and he felt a responsibility to be a part of it. So he walked into a recruiter's office and asked for the airborne infantry. He was formally enlisted on March 2nd, 2006.

Prior to the military, Matt had never flown in his life. At 20 years old, he took his first flight, from Indianapolis to Atlanta, Georgia to go to basic training at Fort Benning. Unlike school, Matt responded immediately to the routine of basic training. He got in the best shape of his life, learned about discipline, and made great groups of friends.

Being an athlete definitely helped. Basic training involved constant running, push-ups, and sit-ups, and Matt could tell immediately who the athletes were in camp. But it wasn't just the physical part of athletics, it was the mental approach. Matt's years of training had taught him that if he focused his attention on something, he could train his body to do it. So when tasks became difficult, or Matt was asked to do something he was unfamiliar with, he knew he could train his body to rise to the challenge.

This approach came in handy when Matt graduated from basic and moved to airborne training. Airborne training involved two weeks of ground training followed by five jumps out of an airplane. This meant that the second trip on an airplane Matt took in his entire life would end with him jumping out of it.

As Matt says, "If you're not scared, something is wrong and you shouldn't be doing it. I remember I was the third jumper out of the door, and I just remember looking down at the ground and I was like, 'This is really going to happen.' Then the green light went on and I took off. I jumped out, the parachute opened, and I thought that was just the coolest thing ever. I hit the ground, we got done, and later that night I called my parents." Matt was an official member of the airborne infantry.

# Afghanistan

His next assignment was Fort Bragg, North Carolina, in the 82nd Airborne Division. Matt joined the unit in August 2006 and was deployed to Afghanistan in February 2007. Some of the soldiers in his unit had already been to Iraq and Afghanistan multiple times, and they tried to share as much as advice as they could before he was deployed. Matt knew to keep his mouth shut, his ears open, and to listen to what was happening around him. He was a in a good platoon, he was trained well, and had prepared as best he could.

Once he was in Afghanistan, "it was hard to distinguish the good guys from the bad guys, but we helped some locals and it was a good deployment." Three months into it, however, Matt found out that the 12-month tour had been extended to 15 months. It was hard to deal with at first, but Matt stuck it out knowing it was part of the job. He completed his deployment successfully, and when he returned to Fort Bragg in May 2007, he was promoted to team leader.

The promotion to team leader was a wake-up call. Rather than being the guy that took orders, Matt was the guy giving the orders. He had a team. He was in charge of three guys, 18 or 19 years old, and the decisions that he made would affect their lives, their family's lives, and Matt's life.

Once again, Matt was able to draw on his experiences in athletics for guidance in a challenging situation. He knew that a winning team has to motivate each other, care about each other, and play their positions effectively. The team was much different now, and the stakes were life and death instead of scores posted on a board. But the underlying fundamentals were the same, and Matt knew how to use them to get the best out of his new team.

Matt's close teammates were Adam, Chase, Jason, Steve and Josh. One Thanksgiving back at Fort Bragg, Matt realized that

Jason had nowhere to go for the holidays, so he drove him back to Indiana for Thanksgiving dinner with Matt's family. Jason, who had grown up in New York and hadn't experienced the rural Midwest, had a blast riding combines and tractors while being unofficially adopted by Matt's family. For Matt, team is family, and family is a team.

Matt's military team was posted in one of the hottest places in Afghanistan. Their job was to search for insurgents planting IEDs and snipers shooting at American soldiers. After the Thanksgiving break, they were deployed back to a dangerous area that required regular patrols day and night.

On December 26th, 2009, Matt was sitting at the platoon base, preparing the gear to go out on night patrol. In the distance he heard the distinct sound of an IED, followed by word that it was Jason that had been hit. Matt ran out to help, but the injury was catastrophic.

Losing one of his teammates was like losing a family member. Matt's commanders informed him that he did not have to go out on patrol that night—he should take the night to regroup with the rest of his team. But Matt knew he was one of the senior guys in the platoon, and he needed to show the team that things were going to be okay. He completed his patrol that night. When he returned, he was informed that Jason had been killed in action.

This was part of the code for a platoon in this area of Afghanistan. As team lead, Matt could have escorted the body home, but he stayed back because he wanted to "try to find the SOBs that did this" to Jason. More than that, Matt knew that his other teammates still needed him by their side. The platoon sent Jason home with another soldier who had been injured.

# June 2nd, 2010

On June 2nd, 2010, Matt had been deployed in Afghanistan for 24 months in a span of four and a half years. He was a veteran leader of a team in another hot area full of insurgent activity. The mission that evening was to complete another night sweep looking for snipers and IEDs.

As Matt recalls it, "I got hit by an IED after covering our exit from a building we called the castle. On the way back to my guys, I stepped on a landmine and got blown up. I was fortunate enough that I hadn't had any of the guys I was in charge of get blown up. The biggest fear I carried with me throughout my time in Afghanistan was getting one of the men I was responsible for killed."

Matt realized he was seriously injured when he was picked up by Adam, Chase, and Steve, all of whom were supposed to be back at base. The three of them had heard the call that Matt was injured and realized that the one medic on patrol might not be there quick enough. They scrambled to escort a doctor and stretcher the half mile to Matt before carrying him back to base.

On the stretcher, Matt tried to keep everyone calm by joking that "I guess I'm getting back before you guys." He remained calm and asked for a thorough accounting of damages, and was told his right foot had been blown off. After being stablized, Matt was transported to Germany and then home to a Defense Department hospital.

His injury required a number of additional surgeries to clean out shrapnel wounds. There is nothing clean about an IED. It is intended to wreak havoc with flesh and bone, and it accomplishes that task with terrible results every time it is detonated near a human being. The routine recovery required a number of every-other-day clean-outs until there was reason to stop searching for more debris, and during that time Matt was kept at whatever level of sedation the condition and pain could tolerate.

# Recovery

Photo courtesy of Matt Kinsey

As with many events in his life, Matt's recovery started with his family. Six days after the attack, Matt was recuperating at Walter Reed Military Medical Center when his family was finally able to see him. As Matt recalled it, "I had Mom, Dad and my brother Mark there, which was really helpful. Mom and Dad struggled with it at first. My brother was very good through the whole thing. We asked a lot of questions, and he kind of helped out. I'd talk to him more than I would Mom or Dad, because they were upset enough watching their son...you know, I didn't have a foot. I had gotten blown up. I had dropped down to 145 pounds."

This was the one period of time when Matt felt sorry for himself. "I didn't look good, you know? I remember one point in time….I was laying in a hospital bed, talking to Mark, and I looked up at him. I just said, 'So what am I going to do, man? I have dreams of maybe playing sports again. I have done well in the military, a good career going. You know, Mark, I'm an athlete. I need to go out and do things. I don't know what I'm going to do.'" His brother told him they they'd figure it out.

And figure it out is exactly what they did. Matt's final surgery was on June 10th, and the next day he went to work with his new team. The team this time was an occupational therapist, a physical therapist, and his family. The mission was getting Matt back in shape. He told them that he didn't care how hard it would be, he was going to regain the life he had before. They agreed to push him as far as he could go.

They started with traditional strength training, physical therapy, and range-of-motion drills. The goal was to get as much of his strength back as possible while the wounds healed. Matt did everything they told him, right down to the smallest detail. Six weeks later, he was ready for his first prosthetic leg.

The idea of a prosthetic is worrying to many, but Matt was very excited. With his parents watching, he took his first tentative steps on his new leg, trying to feel out what this new form of walking was going to be like. But just like after the rotator cuff injury, Matt couldn't allow himself to move slowly for long. As he recalled it, "The leg felt good, and I just took off. I was perfectly fine, like I hadn't missed a beat. I started walking again."

He wore the prosthetic two hours a day, using crutches the remainder of the time. His days revolved around learning to run, getting back in shape, and trying to regain some of the form he had as an athlete. By all accounts, his hard work was paying off, and he was progressing ahead of schedule.

Still, a nagging thought remained in the back of Matt's

mind. Would he ever be able to return to competitive athletics? Running and training brought back many of the positive feelings he remembered, but what Matt really missed was the experience of being on a team. Training alone could bring conditioning, but only teammates could push him back to the place he knew he needed to be.

As he was considering this idea, and wondering what it would be like to be back on a team, Matt met a fellow injured veteran named Josh Wege.

Photo courtesy of Haymarket Joe Photography/Joe Cashwell

Photo courtesy of Captured Memories/Kim Berry

*Chapter 5*

# Joshua "Josh" Wege

## "The Optimistic Warrior"

J osh Wege and Matt Kinsey were completing their re-
habilitations when they heard about the University of
Arizona Disability Resource Center softball camp for
soldiers, Marines and veterans. The idea of the camp was exciting, but it raised a number of questions. What kind of players
would show up? Could a real team emerge from this camp? If
it did, could they be a part of that team?

They mutually decided that the answer to the last two questions was yes, and they set out to prove it. Neither of them
wanted to show up to camp out of shape, so they decided that if
Matt went home to Indiana and picked up his truck they could
do some of the training ahead of time together. By working out
as a pair, and pushing each other to achieve their best, they realized they could improve even faster.

They also decided that the training camp could turn into a
team, and every team needs solid leadership. They knew that
their athletic ambition, character, and drive could be a unifying
element for the group. It wouldn't be easy, and no one could
predict how the team would respond. But, they had a secret
weapon: Josh Wege, the most relentlessly positive, enthusiastic,

and inspiring young man you could ever meet.

Josh was born into a large family led by his mother, Kay, and father, Dave. His siblings included his sister Jess (who generously provided Chapter 3), twin brother Joe, and sisters Jaime and Jordyn. The Weges are a devout Lutheran family who live in Campbellsport, Wisconsin. The parents are educators within the Lutheran private school system, and both had opportunities to have Josh in their class. Both Josh and his parents agree that it was mutually rewarding, which not every family can say about that kind of experience.

Like Matt, Josh was a prodigious athlete as a child. When he was three years old his parents sent him to a gymnastics beginner's class, where they taught the kids how to climb ropes. His parents and instructor looked away for a second, and Josh was 15-20 feet in the air, crying. He had easily figured out how to scamper up the rope, but he was too young too figure out how to climb down.

Josh excelled at whatever was in front of him, whether it was football, baseball, soccer, basketball, or volleyball. On the high school football team he was primarily a defensive back, while in baseball he played left and center field. His favorite part was playing left field with his best friend, Michell Koepke, in center field.

Despite his natural aptitudes, the real genius of Josh isn't necessarily athletic. As a teammate and competitor, Josh has a skill set that stems from what is referred to as the "collective unconscious." The term, popularized by therapists like Milton Erickson and Carl Jung, refers to the ways that people manage their subconscious in response to different experiences. Subconscious forces come into play when someone is in a zero-sum game, such as a tournament, but they can overwhelm the participant if they get consumed by them. Josh has perfect competitive pitch in knowing when cooperative unconscious forces are called for and when the competitive subconscious is required. It is at the heart of how he is able to be a ferocious opponent and supportive teammate simultaneously, and it comes through in every conversation with Josh about any athletic event. Josh has an intuitive understanding of how to be a top-notch teammate.

# Marine Training

During Josh's junior year of high school, he started looking at brochures for the Marines. He was attracted to them because he heard it was the toughest branch to get into, and he always wanted the biggest challenge. So he and a classmate, Nathan Gudex, signed the papers for the Delayed Entry Program and began preparing for Marine entrance testing.

As with Matt, you can see many of the elements of Josh's recovery showing up in his approach to an early challenge. The USMC Physical Fitness Test is grueling, and Josh was not going to show up unprepared. Once a week, he went to the YMCA with the recruiter and ran on the track. Then he would go back to his office and do pull-ups and crunches. A perfect score of 300 is a three-mile run in 18 minutes, then 20 pull-ups and 100 crunches in 2 minutes. When it came time to take the test, Josh got a 297.

Josh was frustrated by the failure to get a perfect score, but he had gained an appreciation for the effort it was going to take. In many ways this helped him in boot camp, since he did not enter with a sense of smug competence or accomplishment. He arrived ready to learn.

The principal goal of Marine training is to purposely move the recruit from some feeling of competence in their past adaptive skills to an awareness that what they don't know (ignorance), combined with what they don't want to know (apathy), can become a lethal cocktail. Josh quickly understood that getting yelled at for seemingly arbitrary reasons served a broader purpose, and he soon learned to be quiet and stay under the radar.

It all clicked for Josh during the last week of boot camp, called Marine Week. During Marine Week, each prospective graduate earns the title of "Marine" through three-day challenge called the "crucible". In San Diego, for example, he participated in stations where past Medal of Honor and Silver Star recipients explained what had happened while Josh reenacted the scene. As Josh tells it, "So if a guy was constantly under enemy fire and he was grabbing ammo cans and bringing them back and forth while risking his life multiple times just to make sure that they could respond to enemy fire, that's what you did. You would get on one side of the hill, just like he was, and you'd compete against the other guys you were with. Every time someone has a turn, they retell the story. I love that the Marines have a proud history. Even in boot camp, you're not just running all day. They actually sit you down to learn our history, the Marine Corps's history, as you're learning to shoot a rifle. You learn about the men who came before you." At the end of the crucible, Josh was awarded his EGA, "Eagle, Globe, and Anchor," the Marine Corps seal, and officially became a Marine.

Once basic training ended, field training began. Josh had already decided to join the military police (MPs), with the eventual goal of joining a S.W.A.T. team once his military career was over. Much of MP training involves police work like checking ID's at the entrance to a base, but it also involves marksmanship and general aptitude testing. Josh finished with the highest shooting scores with both a rifle and a pistol, and was qualified as an expert marksman. He was promoted to Lance Corporal because his physical scores and shooting scores were the best in his class.

## Afghanistan

Lance Corporal Josh Wege was sent to Afghanistan at 19 years old. His deployment was 6 months training the Afghan National Police and the Afghan National Army on patrolling tactics and weapons systems. He taught them how to shoot M16s, conduct basic reconnaissance, and complete patrols.

The natural teammate in Josh found parts of this training unsettling. As he recalls it, "They warn you before you go overseas that the guys who you train will be about 33% Taliban, so never turn your back on them. You just never trusted anybody, so it's a pretty stressful environment to work in, but that was my mission. When I took them on patrol and I was on point it was eerie because you never knew who walking behind you could turn on you, or whatnot. I think your emotions kind of harden when you are there. When I got home it kind of freaked out my family when I got back because they were worried that I wasn't too emotional about anything. I think that was because during war you just learn to deal with things in a different way."

Josh moved to a new assignment in the first deployment training other Afghan soldiers on similar tactics. On his fourth day, he stepped in on a patrol unit for a fellow Marine who didn't have his equipment ready. At the time, Josh didn't give it a second thought.

The job of the patrol was resupplying soldiers with cots, blankets, and food. Josh was in the last armored vehicle of a three-vehicle convoy, an amphibious Light Armored Vehicle with four wheels on each side, useful for traversing the Helmand River, which ran through Josh's Area of Operations. As his patrol was en route, his vehicle rolled over a 200-pound IED, the last tire on the vehicle's left side setting off the pressure plate that triggered the bomb. He found out later that conditions had to be just wrong for the vehicles in front of him to get over it without a scratch and for his to get blown up.

Josh was in and out of consciousness while his platoon worked feverishly to save his life. At times, he didn't know if he would survive. As he remembers it, "Staff Sergeant Killingsworth moved from the front seat and ripped the rear door where I was off its hinges. The Navy corpsman, Mike Camacho, actually put two tourniquets on my legs right away in the vehicle and they pulled me out, although I don't remember being pulled out."

As with Matt and many of the other soldiers in this book, Josh responded with the brand of battlefield humor and composure that often means the difference between life and death. "I remember laying outside the vehicle getting worked on. The funny thing about the story was, I took getting blown up okay— I didn't freak out, and I wasn't screaming like in the movies. But as soon as they started poking me with IVs, that's when I actually ripped it out of my arms. I'm terrible with needles. He gave me the needle again and told me to stop being a wuss, and I was okay again. He kept telling me that I was going to be okay and I said, 'No, I'm not—did you see what happened?' I was trying to joke around a little bit, but I was in less pain than I thought I should be in. It was a stinging pain, but not a screaming out pain. When your adrenaline is pumping and your body is in the shock mine was, it does a good job of protecting itself. They ended up putting four tourniquets on each of my legs because I was bleeding and they couldn't stop the bleeding. I remember the tourniquets because they hurt real bad. Corporal Mathis was there to hold my hand as I went in and out of consciousness. With all that was happening, the simple gesture of Corporal Mathis reaching over to grab my hand was very comforting."

Josh was eventually stabilized and was delivered to a war zone hospital. After immediately thinking of his family, his next thoughts turned to a boot camp story about a Marine named Jason Dunham. While clearing a building, Jason leapt on a grenade to save his teammates, first throwing his helmet and then jumping on it to absorb the blast. He had severe internal injuries, but made it to a hospital in Germany, where he made a phone call to his parents. Jason reassured them that nothing was going to happen to him until he saw his family again. So Jason fought and fought until his family arrived in Germany. Once they arrived, he passed away.

That was the story running through Josh's head as he lay in bed. All he wanted to do was hold on to see his family, but he knew that he could die at any minute.

Josh made it out of Germany and arrived at Bethesda Naval Hospital a few days later. The first day was a blur of searing pain. On the second day, he received a visit from Joe Koffman, a Marine Corps officer who was had been a few classes ahead of Josh in grade school. Finally, on the third day he was able to see his family.

Josh's mother, father, three sisters, twin brother, and brother-in-law all made the trip. As Josh remembers it, "It was one of the best and one of the most painful memories I'll ever have, because I got reunited and my fight to live was almost over. When I was hurt, all I wanted to do was see my family one more time. I can't remember a number of things that happened between the 4th [the day he was injured] and the 11th [the day they arrived] but I do know that when I saw them, I don't think that anyone had told them that I was an amputee."

The idea that he might never walk, run, or play sports again had passed through Josh's mind while he lay in the hospital bed in those early days. But it wasn't until his family arrived that it really sunk in. "I remember laying there and having a tearful re-union with every family member. I had talked with my family on October 5th in Afghanistan. When my twin brother, Joe, came in, he just sat against the wall and didn't say a word. My oldest sister, Jess, tried to be so tough, she said something like 'Hi,' and then she just let it loose. My sister Jordyn came in and she was already crying. Jamie's my middle sister—she's really not good at hospitals and tubes and stuff, so she was freaked out by the hospital setting. The others were trying their best to keep composure."

Josh stayed for a month in Bethesda. His entire family stayed for a week before needing to return to school and work. His twin brother Joe stayed behind. Those who wonder whether twins feel a psychosomatic connection should note that on the day Josh was injured his brother Joe woke up to go to church and found his feet so numb that he couldn't get out of bed. The same day Josh's vehicle rolled over that bomb, Joe couldn't feel his feet. It hasn't happened to Joe before or since.

Once the family cleared out, and Josh was left alone with his brother, he finally let out all the emotions of the experience. As Josh recalls, "That was maybe the first tear I let out as well, because I came from a combat zone and my personality did change." It's tough to imagine someone with a personality as strong as Josh really changing, but he clearly had to absorb a lot of shock to survive both the rigors and trauma of combat. Once he was alone with his brother, he finally let some of the reality sink in.

The next few weeks were filled with the painful routine of clean-up surgeries. According to Josh, "My schedule was pretty much a day of surgery, a wash-out surgery to clean up the tissue and get out the rocks or whatever else was embedded in the legs. You're not even closed up. They just stuff you with something to keep you clean, but you do that a day on and a day off." Josh endured this for about a month.

## Rehabilitation

Josh took his first steps with his prosthetic a month and a half after his injury. He referred to Walter Reed's extensive amputee rehabilitation center as almost like a "factory." There was a regular system that fitted him for prosthetics, checked how his body healed, and tracked his progress. As he healed, he was allowed to progress to core work and light strength training. Two weeks later, he had graduated from crutches to canes, then was weaned off canes over the next two weeks.

The military allows for one key designated person who is allowed to stay with the injured soldier, sailor, Marine, or airman. That person serves as ombudsman, cheering section, connection to the outside, and whatever other useful roles they can work out. For Josh and Joe there was never a question. Joe put aside his personal priorities for nine months so he could do what he knew his brother would have done for him. After the family week, Joe and Josh settled on a plan for getting Josh back to the best shape he could possibly be in.

As Josh remembers it, "My twin brother was there for basically the first 8 months. He stayed with me and was my friend. I was talking to him as he said he's going to be the best man at my wedding. He's just always there for me. He lived with me for 8 months. He dropped school, dropped working, and refused to live with our mom and dad. He was up with me the whole time. My older sister, Jessi, she's a physical therapist and she came out and visited me a couple of times to see my progress. and every time she came out I made leaps and bounds. She got to see little snapshots of where I was going, and it was really neat. My family came out very often. I don't know how many times my best friends came out to visit me just so I could forget about the hospital setting and go to a movie. My job was to spend a year and a half getting better."

One of the problems that Josh experienced early in recovery was that his leg bones tried to grow back, which meant that part of the bone had to be chipped off, forcing him to wait six months to restart his rehab. It was during that time that his relationship with his brother, coupled by visits from other friends and family, helped to break the tedium. Finally, when the bone had healed, he could put on the prosthetics and actively participate in rehabilitation

Josh has a unique prosthetic due to the structure of his legs. His right leg is a bit longer than his left, to the point where he's actually three inches taller with his prosthetic, a decision he could make for himself because his balance is good enough that he can handle the extra height. His prosthetic, made by Össur, is called a modified Cheetah. It looks like a question mark, and when Josh put it on it felt like a carbon fiber spring. It stimulates the calf muscle and fires off better than other prosthetics, which al-

Photo courtesy of Tampa Tribune

lowed Josh to regain more speed and athleticism as his recovery progressed. He has kept in close touch with the company ever since, and they continue to work with him to make sure his "new normal" legs are as responsive as possible.

## A New Challenge

Regaining the ability to run is a great thing, and Josh never takes it for granted. But Josh is a natural athlete. He grew up on ball fields, his formative years were spent playing sports, and he carries the mindset of a great teammate to every challenge he pursues. As he got used to the prosthetic, it was only a matter of time before Josh began to see what competitive team options were available.

The answer came in the course of Josh's relationship with Matt as well as Spanky Gibson, who will be covered in a later chapter. Spanky and Josh were rehabbing together in Washington D.C., and one of ways Spanky kept himself busy was to find out who the new patients were and learn more about their circumstances firsthand. Spanky told Josh about a man named Angel Barcenas, a remarkable double amputee who set the bar for amazing recoveries. Suddenly, Josh had a competitive goal again. He now measured his recovery against Angel, a man he wound up meeting and developing a relationship with. Josh liked how it felt to compete again.

By the time Josh and Matt were recruited to join David Van Sleet's softball training camp, the seeds of a competitive revival were planted. Josh knew that to regain his old form he would need genuine competition as well as a real group of teammates. And once he and Matt were presented with a real team, they embraced the new challenge of preparing to lead. For Josh, that was the final formula for a full recovery—competing, caring, and leading.

Photo courtesy of Captured Memories/Kim Berry

Photo courtesy of Captured Memories/Kim Berry

# Chapter 6

# Saul Bosquez, Jr.

## "I Will Always Be an Athlete"

When Saul arrived in Tucson for spring training camp, he was by himself. Saul is a natural athlete and a pure competitor, so the first thing he did was look around to see if there were any real athletes. Within ten minutes, he had determined that Matt was his athletic equal and Josh was not that far behind. This was going to be a lot of fun.

Saul Bosquez, Jr., known to his friends as Saul, is 28 years old. He has a 3-year-old son, Branden. According to his mother, Janet Dillard, stepfather, John Dillard, and brothers, Jake and Moonie, Saul is a very devoted family member who supported his slightly younger brother Jake and his much younger brother, Moonie, throughout their childhood. This was fortunate for Saul, because Moonie grew up to be 7 inches taller than Saul, and now plays for the Akron University football team.

One of Saul's lifelong characteristics is that he is a Michigan man through and through. Anything from Michigan is better than any other place you could name. The athletes are bigger, the games are more competitive, and all the teams are better. Even the water tastes better in Michigan.

Like many of his WWAST teammates, Saul is a part of the team's "second chance" club. This means that Saul was an athlete with the talent to have a college, or even professional, baseball career, but he never quite took academics seriously enough the first time around. Now, given a second chance on the WWAST, he's tapping into the tremendous athletic gifts he's always had.

John Dillard is not Saul's biological father, having married Saul's mother when Saul was 7. But he grew close to Saul through their shared love, and talent, for sports. John played 3 years of varsity at Detroit Western High School and 4 years varsity at Siena Heights University, so when Saul was growing up he had a lot to offer.

John describes his oldest stepson as one of the most fearless and naturally gifted athletes he's ever been around. "Saul was a natural. He had a natural instinct. I always judge kids' instincts based on if they are afraid of the ball or anything like that. If they are afraid of the ball, that is going to haunt them. They can get over it to a certain extent. He was never afraid of the ball. He always wanted to play catcher, whereas some kids shied away from it. He'd play catcher every game, if you let him. I think innately he knew if he wanted to play every day and wanted to catch, he would have no problem getting on the field—not to mention that he could always hit, too."

The earliest sport that Saul was attracted to was swimming. As a child he had an excellent swimming coach who helped instill solid training habits and taught Saul the basics for how to correctly prepare for athletics. Many of these tips, particularly on nutrition and stretching, have stuck with Saul to the present day.

Saul's attraction to the military began with a group called the "The Young Marines," which he joined when he was eight years old. A man named Steve McGee, known to everyone as Commander McGee, led the group. The Young Marines were similar to the Boy Scouts, in that the groups went on camping trips and earned merits, but they also exposed the children to military customs and discipline. Each family had to buy little uniforms, boots, and a hat. Everything had to be ironed. During local festivals, the Young Marines would march in parades and meet real Marines.

Saul excelled at high school varsity baseball and football. After high school he enrolled in Western Michigan University, but he didn't focus enough on his studies enough to qualify for sports teams. He briefly transferred to a junior college, but that didn't hold his attention either. He eventually returned home after a year and a half.

As with many of his WWAST teammates, Saul's disconnect with school allowed him to pursue a natural attraction to the military. So after returning from junior college, Saul joined the Army. His mom was initially befuddled about the decision, but after she talked to Saul's high school baseball coach she agreed with him that Saul was the kind of guy who enjoyed being part of something bigger than himself. The Army offered a fresh start, a chance to be on a team again, and a second chance to qualify for college funding if he decided to pursue that route one day.

## Cobra Company

Saul was assigned to Cobra Company, 2nd Battalion, 69th Armored Regiment. His primary responsibilities were driving and performing maintenance on a small tank. According to Saul, "It was kind of fun." He particularly liked driving the tank at night with night-vision goggles. Like the other servicemen previously mentioned, he considered mastering the rifle an athletic pursuit and "picked it up instantly." Once in Iraq, his unit was assigned to an outpost that used to be Saddam Hussein's country club. "We had the Tigris River as our backyard."

Saul arrived in Iraq in March 2007. At 8am on August 1, 2007, he was heading back to base in the third vehicle of a four-vehicle convoy. An explosion upended his convoy and knocked Saul partially unconscious.

As Saul remembers it, "It went in slow motion. I checked to see what just happened, and 10 seconds later I felt a burning sensation in my left leg.... As I was trying to get out of the vehicle, that's when I realized that my leg was broken..... My medic, Mack, was the one to put on the tourniquet and put me in the back of a Humvee. Now, here is the strange part. I was on a gurney, but the gurney was wider than the Humvee, so Mack had me lying on my back holding one door while he held the other while he drove me through Baghdad."

When Saul returned from Baghdad to the U.S., he learned that his brain had taken a major concussion from the blast and his leg was going to require an amputation. He was immediately faced with the question of how much of the leg they should save in order to provide for the highest quality of life. Saul quickly learned that the minimum amount was not always the best option, and after a discussion with an army Major who had suffered a similar injury, Saul decided on the more substantial amputation.

It was an impossible position for anyone to be put in, but Saul made the correct choice. Due to the advances in below-the-knee prosthetics, plus the advantage of a clean wound produced by surgical hands, the decision to make a cut higher up the leg yielded a better quality of life for Saul. It was now time to move to rehab.

# *Rehab*

There is an old song called "Something's Gotta Give" that begins with the line, "When an irresistible force such as you meets an old immovable object like me, something's gotta give." In Saul's situation, his irresistible demand to get back all of his former athletic skills was met by the incredibly constant motivation of his therapists, Louise Hessinger (prosthetics specialist) and Annette "Bo" Bergeron (physical therapist). The result was astonishing progress.

Their formula involved 10 hours a week of intense work with both therapists. Unlike many of the other players featured in this book, Saul did not choose to use the buddy system option for rehabilitation. After his mom stayed with him for the first three

Photo courtesy of Saul Bosquez, Jr.

months of his convalescence, Saul elected to pursue the grueling path himself.

Before she left, however, Saul's mom left him with these words: "I saw you take your first steps as a one-year-old, and I will see you take your next steps." That statement brought chills when I first heard it, and it matches the power of any maternal statement I have ever heard in forty years of listening to parents speak about their expectations for their children.

This motivation, combined with the dedication of his healers in residence at Walter Reed Medical Center, were a powerful cocktail for Saul. Without it, there would be no pictures of Saul jumping over anything, let alone hurdles and determined base-runners. As Saul says, "When they asked me what my main goal was in therapy, I said I wanted it to seem like nothing had ever happened to me. I wanted to make it look and seem like I was just like I was four years ago, before I had gotten hurt. And that is what they did."

# The Wounded Warrior Amputee Softball Team

The team has a number of mottos, the most important being "a life without a limb is limitless" and getting accustomed to the "new normal." Saul is a poster child for that philosophy in more ways than one. But he is also a reminder that nothing is so good that it doesn't have something unpleasant associated with it, and nothing is so bad that it doesn't have something good associated with it.

Saul and Matt quickly established themselves as the main-stays of the left side of the WWAST infield. They warm up to-gether, swap tall tales together and enjoy thinking about how it will be to beat yet another team that didn't quite understand the depth of the determination these guys have. It might not be ob-vious at first, but the WWAST is always the visiting team, if only by calculating how many thousands of miles must be flown in order to put together a team of ten or more players. Thumb through the first page of each profile to get the home town, calcu-late the mileage to either New York, Florida, Idaho, Arizona, Michigan, or any of the states and towns visited over the years, and you can see that "just showing up" is an achievement in itself. Add to that the fact that these visitors have probably not seen each other since their last time with the team (which can also vary) and you have a general manager's nightmare. And yet there is sufficient pro-fessionalism and strength of purpose to overcome whatever minor obstacles might be getting in the way of being back on the field.

Saul did return to college, and is set to graduate in December 2014 from Southern New Hampshire University with a degree in Business with a concentration in Sports Management. He has been a regular attendee of as many games as he could get to, and his bat and glove are sincerely appreciated by team and fans alike. The friendship he receives from the other players and the experience of being a part of something bigger than himself keep him traveling throughout the country as a key element to this very special group of military personnel and veterans.

Photo courtesy of Captured Memories/Kim Berry

Photo courtesy of Major League Baseball

Photo courtesy of össur/James Cassimus

*Chapter 7*

# NICHOLAS "NICK" CLARK

## "STILL WATERS RUN DEEP"

The Wounded Warrior Amputee Softball Team has played many places during its three-year history, but the most meaningful experience to Nick Clark occurred inside a penitentiary near Washington, Pennsylvania on the weekend of April 20-22, 2012. In anticipation of the inside-the-walls game, the prisoners presented the team with a gift of $400 raised completely by the convicts. It was a gesture that resonated deeply for many of the players, none more than Nick.

Nicholas "Nick" Clark did not grow up in the stable family environment that many of the other WWAST players were brought up in. Nick's father, Mark, was incarcerated for much of Nick's young life, meaning that Nick only saw his dad when someone would drive him the 4 hours to the penitentiary for visitation. Mark, a self-described drug addict, was incarcerated for 10 years for selling illegal substances.

Mark was not involved in organized crime or anything violent, he was just an addicted person who used drug sales to subsidize his habit. As Nick put it, "Yeah, my dad was a convict. He was in and out of prison most of the time, for mostly drugs and stuff like that. He wasn't a violent offender or anything. He was a great dad when he was out."

Mark is the first one to acknowledge his addiction to substances throughout nearly all of Nick's childhood and adolescence, and he carries with him a strong sense of the consequences of his actions. But Nick and Mark both agree that Mark always cared. According to Mark, "I was an addict and for the most part an absent father. But I would have my family keep me up to date on what was going on in Nick's life and at least once a week, every week I was in jail, I sent Nick a letter telling him about what I had heard and how it was important for him to keep doing the right thing and how proud I was of him and his accomplishments." In the hour or so that Mark described his personal experiences and his relationships with various extended members of the family, he was quick to praise anyone who provided some stability for his son, including his former wife.

Nick was primarily raised in Yakima, Washington with his mom, Julia. Nick's parents have been divorced for most of his life, and he split much of his time between Seattle and Yakama. During his childhood and adolescence he was enrolled in 30 different schools.

When you attend 30 different schools in 12 years, and your father is periodically in jail, adolescence is not the easiest time. Many people in Nick's situation become cynical, violent, or dependent on substances. Nick decided to go a different route. He decided to be a friendly, affable person who gave people a fair shot. While he has never backed down from the fights that came his direction, he never sought them out, either. Where many people would spiral down, Nick decided to develop his own path.

## The Adventurer

Like many of the WWAST members, Nick's path involved athletics. His wide-ranging interests included baseball, basketball, football, soccer, running, snowboarding, and BMX.

Mainly, Nick just loved the thrill of a challenge and the chance to be outdoors.

After quitting high school (though he earned his GED later), Nick worked with his cousin Mitch at a cold storage fishery in Petersburg, Alaska. It was hard work, but it paid well, and the price of living in the area was cheap. The job was for Northwest Seafood, a company that operated a fleet of boats that brought back daily catches of fish. Nick unloaded them, processed them, and cleaned them. As he describes it, "It was one of the most exciting times of my life. I was just a kid on an adventure with my cousin. I was on my own. It was great."

Then came September 11th, 2001. Nick had always had a childhood attraction to the Army, but after September 11th it hardened into something more concrete. He met with an Army recruiter, who recommended the Delayed Entry Program, and spent the next 6 months living with his mother, Julia, while he got in shape. At the end of the six months he reported to Fort Benning, Georgia to begin training.

Nick joined the paratroopers because he thought it was the most challenging job in the Army. His service took him from Fort Benning to Vicenza, Italy, then to Afghanistan. His first posting was in one of the most dangerous areas of the country.

In April, 2007 Nick was posted in a particularly mountainous region. It was a beautiful spring day. Nick was a .50-caliber machine gunner in the very first vehicle of a convoy of about 7-9 vehicles, so in the eyes of the convoy he was the one who had to pull the trigger first. It was a lot of responsibility, but Nick thrived on it.

There was a rock-slide on a mountain road, so Nick's convoy headed over to check it out and see if they could help. On the way there, they were ambushed. Nick's team was pretty far from camp, and the enemy had two fixed positions with two or three combatants at each position. One position was to the left and one was to the right, both at elevations about 100 feet above

Nick. All the fire was coming downhill.

Then the enemy launched rocket-propelled grenades (RPGs), specifically targeting Nick's vehicle and the third vehicle in order to create a choke point. They disabled Nick's vehicle with the very first RPG, which blasted through the cab. Everyone inside was injured by the shrapnel.

Nick sustained a foot injury which later resulted in an amputation. He never lost consciousness, but remembers "white moments" when he had a hard time catching his breath with all the smoke. During one of those moments, a second RPG hit, this time aimed at the third vehicle. Nick and his team realized they had to make their way to the second vehicle before it was too late.

Nick hopped on one leg for 30 meters, with all of his gear, before falling 20 meters short of the second vehicle. A soldier from the second vehicle came out, grabbed him by the vest, and dragged him the rest of the way. Nick credits that soldier, Sergeant Stabley, with saving his life.

The whole time this was happening, the third vehicle was getting ambushed and couldn't aim high enough to shoot back. Nick's roommate, Jacob Lowell, was shot and killed while laying down cover fire. In total, 8 soldiers from Nick's vehicle were seriously wounded.

## Rehab and WWAST

At first the doctors thought that Nick could keep his foot, but once he was flown to Fort Lewis, Washington, he was informed that it would have to be amputated. The question now was how much of the leg Nick could keep. Saul faced a similar circumstance in the last chapter, and it's a quandary that many of the members of the WWAST have had to face. Eventually, the goal of "top quality of life possible" replaced keeping as much flesh and blood as possible, and the larger amputation was selected.

In Nick's case, it was decided that a fusion of the tibia and the shin would provide the best base for a prosthetic. Nick has always been an athlete, so when he was informed that a good base for a prosthetic meant a greater ability to put stress and torque on the leg later on, he knew that was the option for him.

Now Nick had to figure out what his post-rehabilitation life would look like. While rehabbing in Washington, he tried a semester of college, but he found that it still didn't agree with him. As Nick says, "I just wasn't happy with it, and felt like it wasn't something that I wanted to do." Nick was always an athlete and an adventurer, so he began looking around for a new challenge that allowed him to regain that part of his life.

The answer came in a call from David Van Sleet. David found Nick through a prosthetist working at the Seattle V.A. who responded to a request from David looking for guys who played ball before their amputations. Apparently David had a camp in Tucson that Nick might want to attend.

When Nick arrived in Tucson, he knew two of the twenty guys from rehab, but he wasn't sure what to expect from everyone else. Once he started doing some drills and the camp progressed, he realized that all of the guys were intense athletes and competitors. Right off the bat, everyone was trying to outplay one another.

As Nick remembers it, "All of us had been ballplayers before, and then we were in the military together, so we were trying to outdo each other. But that brings out the best in people as far as ability goes. We started to play better and I started to see guys get comfortable." He found the atmosphere of the camp encouraging, and he loved the fact that even though everyone on the field lost an arm or a leg, there were no excuses.

For the first time since his injury, he also started to feel a real sense of community and commonality. Everyone knew what everyone else was going through, so nothing felt out of place. As Nick said, "If I asked someone for a three spliced sock, everyone had a three spliced sock because we were all amputees. It was just special. We had an instant bond because of the combination of softball and the military."

Nick also responded to what he referred to as "the most self-motivating team you've ever seen." The team instantly understood that the key to winning or losing was to care about one another and for each to positively motivate the man next to him. The plays on the field are a matter of individual performance, but all of the preparation is as a team. Nick liked that everyone was used to being relied on, because in the military you have to be at 100% all the time, but each team member also understood that you are only as good as the man next to you.

To cap it off, the team got some cool gear. All of the players appreciated it, but Nick came from a slightly different background. New sports equipment wasn't always handed to Nick as a kid. So when Mizuno offered free equipment, donated courtesy of Mike Candrea, Nick appreciated it. And he remembered everything, whether it was the free Under Armour clothing, University of Arizona gear, or the individualized bats, gloves, and bat bags from Louisville Slugger.

Nick also appreciated the role that David played. As Nick recalls, "He has a military mindset. There was no bull. It was very orderly, and that is the way it should be. During the week, David came up to each guy to talk to them and learn about them as each of us was trying to learn about each other. The group of guys that stood out are still on the team."

Those guys are the reason that Nick is still on the team, too. Nick appreciated the leadership of Josh and Matt, looked up to Spanky (whom we'll meet in Chapter 11), and became best friends with Tim Horton (whom we'll meet in Chapter 8). At the close of camp, Nick remembered thinking that he was going to go back home and pursue a local recreational league, but the memory of the group stuck with him. For a guy from a difficult background, the WWAST was like a new family.

## Coda

Nick's biological family was also changed substantially by the events in Nick's life. When Nick's father Mark heard that his son had been wounded in action, he vowed never to be involved with substances again. Moving forward, he has pledged to be there as a constant presence whenever and however he is needed. Both Nick and Mark expect that this is a promise he will keep.

*To his mother, Nick would like to say,*
*"I love you very much.*
*Thank you for all your hard work."*

Photo courtesy of Missfauxtography Melissa Bergmann

Photo courtesy of REUTERS/Gary Cameron

Photo courtesy of Haymarket Joe Photography/Joe Cashwell

*Chapter 8*

# Timothy "Tim" Horton

## "Tough as a Box of Rocks"

After Tim Horton was given his honorable discharge from the Marines, he enrolled as a 22-year-old freshman in a local school. He wore his prosthetic to class, but his long pants covered it. In a history class, a professor was making comments about the war and said offhandedly that "I wouldn't want any of my children to go there and come back with one leg." Tim remained quiet in the back.

It takes a lot more than an insensitive comment to knock Tim off balance. Given the appellation "tough as a box of rocks" by his Grandpa Tom, Tim is a 5'6" athlete who has always packed a wallop twice his size. As both a middle child and the shorter one, Tim always had to make sure his opponents knew that he was out there ready to compete. Fun for him was the expression on the face of his opponents when they realized just how hard he could hit.

Tim could play pretty much play every sport growing up, but he had a particular fondness for baseball, probably because it is one of the least size-conscious sport of the major American pastimes. He consciously played with a chip on his shoulder, always waiting for the other team to overlook him so he could show them their mistake.

Tim is the only team player whose mother and father were both Marines. In fact, thirteen members of the extended families on both sides served in either the Army, Navy or Air Force. His parents served on the administrative side of the Corps, which he affectionately refers to as "personnel other than grunts" (since the title "grunt" is reserved for those in the infantry who are expected to see action).

Jill and John Horton left the Marines shortly after their first child, Tom, was born. John received the call to serve as a Southern Baptist pastor, and he has been fulfilling that duty for the past 30 years in different locations throughout the central United States. Jill is a certified public school elementary teacher who has gone with her husband to Texas, Iowa, Missouri, Kansas, and Oklahoma. When she found out that her son, Tim, was making plans to join the Marines, her only question was, "Have you prayed about it?" When he told her that he had, and it was the right thing to do, that was that.

Tim is very proud of the fact that his parents are still married after over 30 years. He doesn't condemn others who are different from him, but he feels comfortable knowing that there is a fundamental order in his family structure. Their guidance, coupled with strong religious beliefs, formed a structure that Tim could lean on whenever challenging times arose in his life.

In his youth Tim played football, baseball, and even basketball. While moving frequently interfered with particular sports seasons, he did make his high school baseball team his senior year. He modeled the hard-working style of his game after his grandfather, Tom Hall, who Tim says "is the hardest-working man I have ever met in my life. He's 74 and he's a source of inspiration to me. He works three jobs, one as a roofer. He was a heck of an athlete. He was put in his high school Hall of Fame."

Tom also set an early example of how to deal with pain and adversity. One day, while Tim and his family were hunting, Tom broke his finger. Instead of leaving for the hospital, Tom just started pulling on it. He never got it fixed, and it's still crooked to this day. As Tim says, "I just laugh every time I look at it. I am just like that. Maybe a little dumb that we didn't get something fixed, but that's the way I am."

## Marine Training

If Tim had been a bit bigger, he says that he might have liked to play college sports. Since he always knew that he was going to try his hand in the Marines, he decided to go into the Delayed Entry Program. Like many of the WWAST, he was a natural fit for basic training.

As Tim remembers it, "I wasn't big on the drill part of it. But the physical stuff, I was actually prepared for, so I thought it was easy. My family's mentality was that you completed what you started, so that was how I went about being a Marine." Tim trained at Camp Pendleton before signing up for mortar training with a weapons platoon.

Once mortar training was complete, Tim's group of mortar men, machine gunners, and assault men were attached to three infantry platoons. Later Tim was assigned to Fox Company 2nd Battalion, 5th Marine Regiment, First Marine Division, which at that time was known as the most decorated unit in the Marine Corps.

In September 2004, Tim's division was sent to Iraq. At first they defended a makeshift post where they were mortared fairly frequently. He completed missions to clean up the city he was in and protect the Iraqi people from insurgents, all of the time either patrolling on foot or driving a Humvee. The only mortar rounds he launched were illumination rounds to light up the sky so his team could see what was going on.

Tim's mission ended on February 5th. As Tim remembers it, "It was a day like any other day. We were in our Humvees and I was driving the rear vehicle. As the last Humvee in the mobile patrol, it was our job to provide security so the rest of the Humvees could pass without incident. So the first one passed and an IED went off—it mostly got Iraqi civilians. It basically exploded underneath the engine—a lot of times these were suicide missions—so our unit finds that people are dead after that happened. I remember my ears ringing at that point because the IED had been pretty close, and so my squad leader said, 'Get in, get in, get in. Back up, back up.' So I'm backing up, and the next thing you know, a second IED goes off under our vehicle. That's when I got hit. From this point there are parts and pieces I remember and parts and pieces I don't. The force of the explosion knocked me out, and when I came to, a Corpsman was asking me questions about my dog tags. As I was loaded onto the helicopter, the last words I heard, in a country twang, were, 'You're gonna be alright.'"

Tim was injured not far off the base, so they immediately responded with a Navy Corpsman. Tim credits the rapid response with saving his life. He was then transported to Germany, where he was stabilized for a broad variety of injuries to his arms, legs, shoulders, hands, and face. He had to wear a patch on his left eye for the initial period of recuperation.

Once he was stabilized, Tim was finally able to call his mother and father. His fingers and wrist were broken, so he had to hold the phone up with his shoulder. As Tim recalls, "I ended up dropping the phone and had to call for the nurse. My arms were in foam blocks because my left wrist and both elbows were broken."

Tim was taken to Bethesda, MD, where all his surgeries began. In Bethesda he still had his legs, and the doctors were primarily concerned with working to get the shrapnel out. But on February 25th, the doctors decided that the cleanouts were not going to be enough, and they would have to cut Tim's leg off.

That was the first and only time that Tim's mom ever saw her son shed a tear. Tim doesn't dwell on that day, except to remember that there was a movie on TV that evening starring Dan Aykroyd where he pops off his leg. Tim turned to his mom and told her that he was going to be able to do that.

Despite his staunch determination, however, Tim was fully aware of the changes that had rapidly occurred as the result of his injury. Tim is not a naturally big man to begin with, and when he's in top Marine shape he usually weighs around 155 pounds. By the time he started therapy, he was down to 111. In addition, while Tim was preparing to start some of the same leg rehab that other WWAST members have gone through, his challenge was made more difficult by the raft of injuries across the rest of his body. He had 8 surgeries on his face alone while preparing to be fitted for a leg prosthetic.

After a period of improvement, Tim, like Josh, experienced a setback during the bone growing phase. As the bone grew back, it began causing intense pain whenever he put pressure on it, resulting in new surgery and a restart of rehabilitation. Throughout this time period Tim had to keep reminding himself that one day, no matter how far away it seemed, he would be back to his old self.

## Wounded Warrior Amputee Softball Team

When asked to describe his teammates, Tim speaks in paragraphs rather than just sentences or descriptive words. The team matters to Tim. He looks up to the other players, draws inspiration from their efforts, and enjoys every minute of his time on the field.

Tim knew that the training camp could be meaningful as soon as he first heard about it, and like many players, he wanted to show up prepared. Tim's father reached out to a college baseball coach at Cameron College, Todd Holland, to see if Tim could have a chance to practice with the team. Coach Holland agreed, and Tim got to work.

As Coach Holland remembers it, Tim worked harder, by far, than any one of his varsity players. He had some initial difficulty getting up to speed in both offensive and defensive skills as an outfielder, but after a relatively awkward first week he continued to get the hang of it. By the second week, Tim was able to keep up with most of the other players.

Coach Holland made it a point to not cut Tim any slack, which Tim appreciated. It allowed Tim to dig as deep as possible and grit out the challenging moments on the field that can't be simulated in an easy practice. In return, the team got an up-close experience with an inspiring athlete. As Coach Holland recalls, "We still remember how that guy hustled, how he did whatever task needed to be done, like shagging balls or getting the field ready for play. Everything was important and appreciated. It was an honor and a pleasure having him with us for those weeks."

When time arrived in Tucson for WWAST camp, he brought the same competitive fire with him. The preparation, combined with Tim's natural drive, paid off. He was one of the most prepared players in camp, and he has gone on to be one of its most productive. He may be one of the smallest, and he may have faced some of the most serious injuries, but Tim's drive, grit, and passion put him back on the field where he belonged.

Photo courtesy of Haymarket Joe Photography/Joe Cashwell

Photo courtesy of Captured Memories/Kim Berry

Photo courtesy of Haymarket Joe Photography/Joe Cashwell

Photo courtesy of Captured Memories/Kim Berry

# Chapter 9

# Robert "Bobby" McCardle

## "A Gentleman"

When Bobby was lying injured on the battlefield, his first thought was that he wanted to see his wife, Stephanie, again.  He finally got to see her, in a hospital bed back home, but when he did he wasn't even able to say hello.  His jaw was severely broken in the explosion and had to be wired shut.  So Stephanie sat by his bed every day for 14 hours and did the speaking for both of them.

Stephanie's response wasn't the kind of family experience that Bobby was used to.  Bobby McCardle is a member of the group of WWAST players that had a non-traditional childhood, with various caretakers alternating custody.  He often moved between different family members, and even spent three years with Child Protective Services.

The most consistent family was his father's parents.  Bobby's grandparents lived in Hales Corners, Wisconsin, and from the 5th grade on, Bobby had a place with them near his father.  His dad's sister Pat was always around to look out for him and give much-needed motherly guidance.  When Bobby got to high school, he lived with his mother's brother Scott, who kept him on track through a very difficult time.  By his senior year, he lived independently in an apartment that he shared with a friend.

When you are paying your own rent at that age, you develop a different kind of worldview. From an early age, Bobby created a line that wasn't worth crossing. In his words, "Certain kids I could always get in trouble with. All in all, I got into the right amount of trouble and stayed out of the right amount of trouble. There were always options for me to turn out differently, I guess, but it didn't work out that way."

Bobby also developed a quick understanding of the importance of a paycheck. He got his first job at 14 at a grocery store, and he landed a second job shortly after, doing carpentry, plumbing, and electric work as a construction apprentice. He worked at both jobs until the day he joined the Marines.

When he had the chance to play sports, Bobby was very good. Baseball was his favorite sport, and when he got the chance to attend baseball camps and receive coaching, he developed quickly. But work cut into sports, at times preventing him from playing on the high school team. Despite the obstacles, he was still able to earn a starting spot as a senior and have a productive year.

## *Joining the Marines*

Once he joined the Marines, all Bobby wanted was the infantry. He was able to attend boot camp within a month of signing up, and when he got there he responded immediately to the structure, discipline, and security. He thought the military was a well-oiled machine, and he respected the way they did things.

One element he particularly appreciated was the senior-junior platoon, where he was paired with experienced members tasked with developing him. As Bobby says, "The magic of a senior-junior platoon is that you get treated bad for a purpose—so you take your job seriously, as life and death depend on it. There is a method to their madness. And the greatest thing I have ever learned was never to take anything personally...I've got nothing but praise for how I was prepared to do my job in combat."

Bobby graduated from basic training as a mortar man and was assigned to the 1st Marine Expeditionary Unit (MEU). His unit was initially deployed overseas, but returned home after they were not needed in active combat. On the next deployment, he was transferred from a mortar platoon to a mobile assault platoon headed for Iraq. His strong work to that point earned him a leadership position and his own squad.

His squad's primary job was spotting IEDs. They had received most of their training on spotting IEDs in urban environments, but in Iraq they found themselves near a lot of dirt or "make-your-own" roads. As Bobby recalls, "It was definitely a curve ball thrown at us." But Bobby and his team adapted quickly, and his unit served with distinction.

In the middle of the deployment, while he was serving in the lead vehicle in an IED patrol, Bobby's convoy was hit by an IED. The explosion was so powerful that parts of the engine of his vehicle were found a mile away. He initially sustained a severe concussion, but his team was able to quickly extract him from his vehicle and transport him out of harm's way. He was on a helicopter within 15 minutes, a feat that Bobby credits to the training and rapid response of his squad.

Part of that response required caring, humor, and quick thinking during the moments while Bobby was waiting for the helicopter. He asked his Corpsman for a shot of morphine to help with the violent pain in his injured leg, but his team knew that you don't give morphine to someone with a significant head injury. As Bobby struggled with the pain, his team worked to keep him engaged and distracted as best they could.

As Bobby recalls that one of his good friends, Jesse Klotz, came back, took a look, and told him to stop acting like a wuss. "As soon as he started talking crap to me, that's when I settled down. It was better than morphine. It was exactly what I needed. He just calmly came up and tapped me and told me to stop acting. All I could do was laugh. Then we said a prayer together and I waited for the bird."

# Rehabilitation

The bomb shattered Bobby's hip, elbow, and jaw. He lost several teeth and part of his leg. He was sent to Baghdad for a week to complete initial surgeries, and then was transferred stateside. Initially, he couldn't eat, due to the severely broken jaw, and his mouth had to be wired shut.

The wired jaw made it impossible for Bobby to speak, a fact that made already difficult meetings with loved ones even more trying. He was met immediately at the hospital by his wife, Stephanie, who came to the hospital at 8 a.m. every morning and stayed until 10 p.m. every night. As Bobby remembers it, "Things were just not as painful when she was there. She made everything a lot easier. I had less frustration when she was there. Just the fact of her coming in the room would make the pain and frustration and everything else go away—just by her being there."

Stephanie helped Bobby with every element of his initial recovery. She helped keep his wired jaw clean, met constantly with doctors and nurses, and talked to Bobby for hours even though he could only write back in response. Bobby and Stephanie had married between his first and second deployment, and both were only 20 years old when he was injured. Her response is a testament to their connection as well as a remarkable statement on her maturity, intelligence, and capacity for caring.

Bobby and Stephanie's luck began to improve when they received some unexpected support from Jack and Barbara Lyon, a couple they met at the hospital. Jack was a Silver Star veteran of the Vietnam War, and Jack and Barbara had been making a regular practice of coming to the hospital and meeting with wounded veterans. They could tell immediately that Bobby and Stephanie were a special couple in a challenging situation.

As Bobby remembers it, "What Jack and Barbara did for us

was monumental, because one thing a vet knows is how to listen to another vet. Vietnam-era guys had walked in our shoes before. Regarding the initial PTSD (Post-Traumatic Stress Disorder) stuff, he was the one guy who you could talk to who knew what you were going through." On Stephanie's end, Barbara had a wives' group that met regularly to discuss the issues associated with providing constant care to an injured loved one. It was tough for Stephanie, because she hated the idea of leaving Bobby's side, but Barbara convinced her to attend.

Stephanie came to that first meeting with a little hesitation, but quickly formed lasting friendships with the other young wives. She listened intently to other people's challenges, and she shared her experiences and feelings while giving total support to those in need. Her ability to be available for the other wives, in spite of her own needs, was appreciated deeply by everyone in the group.

For their part, Jack and Barbara took immediately to the young couple. As Barbara remembers it, "Both were very warm and welcoming… and very young! Stephanie was sitting right on the side of the bed, as close as possible to Bobby. They were happy for the visit, but I could tell Stephanie did not want to leave his side. She was totally dedicated to Bobby—to caring for him, to keeping 'eyes on' at all times."

Barbara still thinks of her often, and remains struck by the qualities that Stephanie exhibited during this challenging time. As Barbara says, "Stephanie has all the qualities I would want my own daughter to have—inner strength, devotion, dedication, trust, a positive outlook on life, and confidence… We are separated by distance now, but I will always hold a special place in my heart for Stephanie. A big smile comes to me whenever I think of her. Just knowing that we will always have a deep connection is a gift beyond words. She is an amazing young woman—she is love."

# Wounded Warrior Amputee Softball Team

Bobby's convalescence was complicated by the fact that he only had one kidney, and was therefore was not healing as quickly as he had hoped. His leg eventually required amputation, and he began the arduous rehabilitation process that many of the WWAST have completed. Through it all, Stephanie was there for motivation, support, and guidance.

Part of this support was understanding that Bobby needed an athletic challenge to recapture the active part of his personality that had been lost with his injury. Bobby and Stephanie had always envisioned Bobby running around in the backyard and playing sports with their children, but this basic aspiration was now compromised. If Bobby was going to play in the backyard with his kids, he would first have to remember how to play on his own.

So when the call from David Van Sleet came, Bobby and Stephanie knew it was the right choice. Bobby is a family man at heart, and he didn't approach the spring training with the competitive fervor of other WWAST members. The training camp was a chance for him to get back in shape, and when he played well enough to make the initial traveling squad, he knew he had regained a measure of himself that he needed.

Bobby loves being with his WWAST teammates, and he plays his hardest every game. He has developed some great friendships, particularly with Nate Lindsey, who is profiled in the next chapter. But what he most appreciates is how the WWAST has allowed him to regain an element of himself that he could share with his family. After growing up in challenging childhood circumstances and living through a traumatic injury, Bobby's goal is to build a healthy, caring, and stable life for Stephanie and their children. The WWAST is an important part of making that happen, and he is forever grateful.

Photo courtesy of Captured Memories/Kim Berry

Photo courtesy of Captured Memories/Kim Berry

Photo courtesy of Haymarket Joe Photography/Joe Cashwell

*Chapter 10*

# Nathaniel "Nate" Lindsey

## "A Consummate Appreciator"

W hen David Van Sleet put together the original roster of 20 players to invite to Arizona for spring training, Nate Lindsey was number 21. Some players would be slighted by this, but not Nate. He comes from a school of thought that understands that when certain opportunities close, other opportunities open up, and all we can do is be ready. So when a player dropped out of camp, Nate showed up ready to compete.

Nate grew up in De Kalb, Illinois, where he was raised by his parents alongside his two brothers, Nick and Pete. His mother, Ann, is an English teacher at Kishwaukee College, and his father Scott originally worked at a lumber yard before working at a library.

Nate, like most of the other players mentioned throughout the book, was an outstanding athlete growing up. His favorite sports were wrestling and baseball, which he was initially attracted to because his dad's family was full of avid baseball fans. Growing up, Nate enjoyed fishing and camping with his family, and appreciating as much of the outdoors as possible. Nate was a sophomore in high school when 9/11 occurred, and it made him angry enough to want to do something personally about it. So, at 17, during his junior of high school year, he joined the Army. He signed up for the Delayed Entry Program, and was stationed in Fort Lee, Virginia before being deployed to Panama, where he served as a truck driver.

Driving a truck in the Army is a dangerous, complicated responsibility, but Nate excelled at it. For his next deployment he was sent to Iraq to drive a 22-wheel flatbed tractor-trailer. He also shared defensive responsibilities with other soldiers, often securing either a .50-caliber machine gun or an M240B machine gun (7.62mm). His first deployment was a 10-month tour from February 2005 to November 2005.

The second deployment, from June 2006 to August 2007 entailed similar responsibilities as the first. Nate drove long haul trucks, supported by companies of Humvees, and when the support companies were unavailable, Nick would man the turret. His convoys repeatedly took heavy fire and were often targeted by explosive devices. As Nate remembers it, "In the first tour, you got blown up, you got a concussion, and you went back the same night or the next night, so it just was the way it was. You couldn't call it normal, but it was what we regularly experienced. We always got hit by small arms fire, but fairly regularly we got hit by something bigger." In the course of this service Nate was promoted to Sergeant, referred to as E-5.

One night, on a routine convoy, Nate's spotlight was broken, so he used a SureFire flashlight to shine stopped trucks out of the convoy's path. In the course of this duty, an IED went off ahead, allowing Nate only enough time to get his head down before the impact hit the truck.

After applying a tourniquet and then receiving help from his fellow soldiers he sat on the truck's stairs and waited for the helicopter to arrive. Nate was transported to base before being sent to Germany for recovery.

# Recovery

The extent of Nate's injuries allowed no choice besides amputation to a point below the elbow where he had a chance to heal. Arm injuries are a different form of challenge than the leg injuries experienced by many of the other WWAST members, but both injuries require a lot of effort early in the recovery process. So, immediately after surgery, Nate began re-learning how to use everything in his arm below his elbow.

In the leg injuries covered in the book thus far, the primary points in recovery involve re-learning how to walk and establishing new patterns for how to put weight on the leg. Arm injuries are not weight-bearing, but they involve small muscle rehabilitation and the rebuilding of hand-eye coordination. This is grueling, time-intensive work that requires teaching yourself all the basic functions of how your arm operates, including unconscious functions that are typically taken for granted.

Nate's right arm was injured, so his first major objective was teaching his left hand, wrist, arm and shoulder to do many of the tasks that his previously dominant right arm had done. This is painstaking work, but Nate was fueled by constant thoughts of his young daughter Jackie, whom he got to see shortly after his injury. Nate always believed that a father needs to be able to play catch with his children, but he wasn't sure if that was an option for him anymore. He was going to rehab as hard as he could to find out.

# Wounded Warrior Amputee Softball Team

One of Nate's inspirations was Jim Abbott, the one-armed MLB pitcher who threw a no-hitter against the Cleveland Indians while he was a member of the New York Yankees. Abbott was born without a right hand, and his efforts showed the world that

Photo courtesy of Captured Memories/Kim Berry

a one-armed man could succeed in what was thought to be an exclusively two-armed sport. So in the back of his mind, Nate knew he could get back on a field one day.

When Nate was named an alternate to the WWAST, he treated it as an honor. Prior to camp, he spent months with Dave L'Hirault, Francisco Ramirez and Tim Kilty to prepare for his new lefty assignments. According to Dave, "Basically, he brought a bat and glove and a bunch of balls and we went out to a field to hit balls to him. He fielded balls for about a month and a half, about 3 days a week, from an hour to an hour and a half. He was a bit frustrated for the first three or four times, but he quickly got the hang of it and after a week you could definitely see improvement."

After a while, Nate could make regular contact with predictable results. Throughout the training, he kept up a love for the game that guided his improvement. He appreciated everyone who went out of their way to help him improve, and he never took for granted the extra effort others were putting in. As Dave remembers, "It was always easy to be out there with him, because it was clear what he wanted to achieve and he was willing to give it his best."

Nate's WWAST teammates are glad that he stuck with it and made the squad. For his part, Nate enjoys spending time with his teammates, visiting new places all over the country, and regaining an element of his old identity that the injury had taken. The WWAST provided the challenge he needed to get himself back to a level he knew could get to. Today he enjoys spending time with his wife Courtney and kids Jackie, Miles and Flinn. He can play catch with his children, or anyone who asks, with no problem at all.

Photo courtesy of Captured Memories/Kim Berry

Photo courtesy of Captured Memories/Kim Berry

*Chapter 11*

# WILLIAM "SPANKY" GIBSON
# "A MARINE"

## "WHAT'S IN A NAME?"

President George W. Bush was preparing to commemorate the fifth anniversary of the invasion of Iraq, and his speech cited the bravery of a Marine Gunnery Sergeant named William Gibson. The President had a problem, however. The speech referred to Gibson as "Spanky." This concerned the President, who did not want to refer to a decorated Marine disrespectfully, so he called Sergeant Gibson. Gibson put the President at ease by telling him what he tells everyone: Just call him Spanky.

It's a nickname that William Gibson has carried with him for a long time. George "Spanky" McFarland was a beloved member of the "Our Gang" comedy show, and when William showed up at boot camp, a drill sergeant thought it was the perfect nickname to fit the off-the-wall personality of the recruit in front of him. Few on the WWAST would disagree. Every teammate has a story of the larger-than-life funny guy who makes sure that everyone in the room, and on the field, is staying loose and having a good time.

There is another side of Gibson, however, that does not have a nickname. That is because you do not need a nickname to describe a highly decorated career Marine who has spent twenty-two years in hot spots ranging from Desert Storm to Somalia. You do not need shorthand to describe someone who came back from an above-the-knee amputation to return to active duty in Iraq. You just refer to him as "Master Sergeant."

## Growing Up

Spanky Gibson was born in Claremore, Oklahoma, the only son of Gene and Mary Gibson. As a kid he wrestled, hunted, and did as much as he could outdoors. As Spanky remembers it, "I spent a lot of time by myself just hunting squirrels, hunting rabbits, walking around the woods, etc. I jumped my bike over my mom's Pinto, stuff like that. It was a relatively easy, pretty fun childhood."

Spanky played baseball until the seventh grade and participated in youth league football. In junior high, he wrestled at the 70-80 lb. weight class, and in high school he wrestled in the low 100's. He was relatively undersized, but he was a tenacious competitor.

His inspiration for the Marines was his grandfather, a 30-year veteran with an accomplished history of service. As Spanky recalls, "My grandfather was probably my number-one inspiration to join the Marines. I joined up with my friend Jon, but he wanted aviation, and I wanted infantry so I could shoot guns. I wanted to be everything I saw about the Marines. I wanted to be the guy painting my face, playing around in the woods. That's what I ended up doing for a good majority of my life."

## Career Soldier

Spanky Gibson is a career Marine. He has 20 meritorious citations, including the Purple Heart and the prestigious Navy/Marine Corps Commendation medal with "V" device given for Valor in the face of an enemy combatant. He earned them serving in areas all over the world, including Operation Desert Storm, Operation Iraqi Freedom, and several hot spots in Africa.

In 2006, during his third tour in Iraq, Spanky was leading foot patrols in Ramadi when a sniper's bullet hit his left knee. It shredded the tendons, disintegrated his kneecap, and severely buckled his leg. A group of Navy SEALS were also on patrol, and they pulled him to safety in a nearby courtyard. Spanky continued returning fire at the snipers as he was being dragged away.

Unlike many of the other WWAST members, who experienced their traumatic injuries at a young age, Spanky was 35 at the time of his injury. He had served in multiple theaters and in a variety of combat environments, so he wasn't in shock when the bullet hit. He knew the damage was bad, but he was primarily focused on getting the other Marines out safely.

Doctors at a nearby combat hospital initially tried to save it, but eventually they were forced to amputate. For Spanky, the hardest part wasn't the amputation; it was realizing he was leaving his Marines back in Iraq. As he was transported out of the country, his first thought turned to how he could get back.

Less than a year after his injury, Spanky had fully recovered and been fitted with a prosthetic leg. He began working exhaustively to regain his athleticism, starting with running, and he eventually moved to biking, swimming, and even skiing. Within eighteen months, Spanky was walking with only a barely perceptible limp.

Unlike many of the other players, however, he did not just want to get back on a ball field. He wanted to get back to Iraq. But Spanky was an above-the-knee amputee, and military regulations prohibited his redeployment. Gibson refused to give up the dream, however, and trained relentlessly for triathlons to prove that he was in peak physical shape. One day, while competing at the Escape from Alcatraz Triathlon in 2007, Spanky had a serendipitous run-in.

James Mattis, a Marine General who later served as the head of U.S. Central Command, was in San Francisco for the race. Mattis asked Spanky if there was anything he could do for him, and Spanky told him he wanted to redeploy. After a number of bureaucratic hurdles, a year later Spanky became the first above-

Photo courtesy of Chris Poore, Cashman Productions

the-knee amputee in the history of the U.S. military to go back into active duty. The Marines and the Army have since lifted the restrictions on above-the-knee amputees, and a total of six, including Spanky, have redeployed.

## *Wounded Warrior Amputee Softball Team*

Spanky Gibson is one of the elder statesmen of the WWAST. He is older than the other players, and lacks some of their athletic pedigree. But the respect, loyalty, and affection he generates is unparalleled. Every player has a Spanky Gibson story.

Sometimes the story is about a player feeling uncomfortable, and Spanky putting them at ease. Other times it is a player doubting how much of themselves they could regain after injury, and Spanky refusing to let them acknowledge any other option besides a full recovery. Most of the time it is about Spanky generously sharing his time, or an inspirational moment, with anyone who needs one.

For Spanky, the team serves a number of purposes, the most important being the opportunity to continue connecting with fellow warriors. He loves showing teams and fans around the country that the amputations did not get in the way of team members living a full and healthy life, and he encourages players at every turn to set their goals as high as possible. When the message comes from a decorated hero who broke down the walls prohibiting amputees from returning to active duty, it carries a special amount of weight.

Photo courtesy of Lisa Macias

Photo courtesy of Haymarket Joe Photography/Joe Cashwell

# Chapter 12

# MANUEL "MANNY" DEL RIO
## "MAKING THE MOST OF
## SECOND CHANCES"

Manny Del Rio understands second chances. His father, Jose, was a 20-year-old baseball player trying out for the Pittsburgh Pirates Minor League system when he was randomly shot in the back during a drive-by shooting. Jose didn't get a second chance.

Several years later, Manny was serving in the United States Navy when his leg was crushed in a catastrophic injury. For many service members, this could have been the end of their dreams and aspirations. But Manny knew that he was still alive, and he still had a chance. And that was all he needed.

## *Growing Up*

Manny Del Rio is the eldest son of Elpidia and Jose Del Rio. His father came from Mexico to California in his teens, and he received his citizenship when Manny was a child. His father played ball recreationally, and was always focused on his son's athletics.

Manny's family worked hard, but he does not come from a privileged background. The family's one car was used by Manny's father to go to and from work, so when Manny went to games he would often leave two hours beforehand so he could ride the bus with his mom. This kind of commute would tire out other players, but not Manny. He loved the game, and his teams, too much.

Manny played catcher, a position that requires natural leadership and communication skills. Manny has an abundance of both of these qualities. He was always the first player on the field to let the guys know that even if they were down, or the pitcher was struggling, they just needed to relax and take it one pitch at a time. The team's second chance was just around the corner.

Manny was a light-hitting catcher, so he knew his main job with the team was working with the pitcher. It was a role that Manny understood intuitively. As he recalls, "The pitcher is here because he is the best one to get the job done now. Our job was to help his confidence and be ready to make the plays behind him. And when we came to bat, each hitter was there to provide our best chance to win. Cheer him on and let him know how much confidence we had in his ability to get it done."

In high school, Manny bagged groceries at a local supermarket. The job provided a much needed salary, as well as an opportunity to apply his team-first attitude in a productive way. As he recalls, "It wasn't much effort for me to help them out to their car or help them get something. Thinking back, I really appreciate that I got that opportunity to understand what it was to earn my $80 or $100 per week. That's the money I used in my junior and senior years for gas and to pay for my own insurance."

Manny worked all day on Saturdays, which meant that his commute home brought him by some dangerous areas during relatively late hours. There were two gangs near his work, and the streets were poorly lit. But Manny always gritted through. He put his hands in his pocket, put his head down, and kept walking home.

# U.S. Navy

Manny decided to join the military right before his high school graduation in 2004. He believed that the country had given him and his family a number of terrific opportunities, and now the country was at war. Something in Manny made him want to be part of something bigger than himself, and he knew he could make a difference.

Manny also had a cousin in California who served as a role model for military life. His cousin had played high school baseball, joined the Army, and returned home to become a police officer in the LAPD. Manny wanted the same dream, except he wanted the Navy instead. He liked the idea of traveling to far-reaching places while being responsible for sensitive equipment, and he enjoyed the diversity he experienced during recruitment.

Basic training in the Navy does not involve the same level of physical training as the Army or Marines. There is still an intense level of fitness that is expected, but the focus is more on how each sailor is expected to operate systems. The Navy expects each recruit to focus intently on their technical training and academics, as every system is highly technical.

Manny went from basic training in Great Lakes, Michigan, to Pensacola, Florida, for aviation training. His first deployment was on an aircraft carrier called the USS Kitty Hawk, where he was in charge of directing all of the aircraft on the flight deck. He also assisted senior airmen with activities like tying down the jets with chains.

He commendably served two deployments on the carrier, and he was sent back for a third deployment in late October of 2005. His career was proceeding very well. He passed a number of required exams, and had reached the point where he was close to E-4 status, a promotion that resulted in him being assigned a trainee. He also was able to cross the equator, a tradition that promoted from "pollywog" to "shellback" status in the Navy community.

Manny was in the course of instructing his new trainee when a dramatic series of events unfolded. Manny and his team were towing a jet on one of the elevators, a process that moves the jet by a tow bar hooked up to a tractor. There was one person to the left of the jet, and Manny and his trainee were to the right. All of a sudden, the tractor came to a stop. Before they were allowed to start again, Manny needed to check underneath the jet and make sure that everything was okay. But instead of continuing in the direction it was going, the jet began moving the other way, and as Manny was stepping back out he was pinned down. The entire jet rolled over his left and right legs.

At first he didn't feel pain, as his body went into shock. His immediate concern was being crushed entirely by the jet, but he was able to reach out and crawl forward to pull his midsection away from the tire. When the plane finally stopped, it was literally parked on Manny's lower body.

The crew chief rushed over immediately and began working to get Manny out. It took 25 excruciating minutes for the crew to lift the plane off his leg and several more to pull him underneath it and get him on a stretcher. As Manny was being carted off, his last words to the team were, "I'm going to miss you guys. Tell my family that I love them. Everything's going to work out. If anything goes wrong, I love you guys and thank you."

Manny was taken from the ship to the nearest hospital, which was in Okinawa, Japan. His legs were so badly damaged that the doctor needed to amputate his right leg below the knee. His left leg had swollen to 5 times its normal size. He needed a muscle transplant from his back to support the remaining bone in his leg, as well as a skin graft from both thighs in order to salvage the stump.

His initial reaction was complete shock, followed by concern. As Manny remembers it, "What am I going to do now? I have no experience aside from just graduating from high school.

I'm in training here in the Navy, but other than that I have no college degree. I don't have anything. Who is going to want to hire me now?"

## Recovery

After the initial despair, Manny collected himself and began the long process of getting better. He knew that the adversity was unlike anything he had ever faced before, but he knew he had to face the next series of challenges as best he could. Once he was stabilized, he was transferred from Japan back to the Balboa Naval Medical Center in in San Diego, and rehabilitation began.

During his stay in San Diego, he met two people who were instrumental to his recovery. Alex Morales, a double below-the-knee amputee, and his wife Shawn helped Manny understand that he was beginning a road to recovery that would end with a high quality of life. He just needed to stick with it, rehab as hard as he could, and never stop believing in himself.

He was then transferred to Brooke Army Hospital in San Antonio, Texas where he had another fortunate encounter. During roll call he noticed Alex Del Rio, a Marine Staff Sergeant E-6 who was a double below-the-knee amputee. Alex, who had already been recuperating at the hospital for two months, turned out to be Manny's second cousin, and Alex's family lived in San Antonio.

The cousins formed an instant bond. Manny was treated by Alex's mother, Clarisa, father, Jose, and their other sons, Louis, Jose, and Gabriel, as a new member of the family, and for a year and a half the cousins worked out together. Manny had the experience of developing a close relationship with an older cousin guiding his recovery. Alex, for his part, cared deeply about Manny and wanted to do everything he could to help him recover. When Manny later married his wife, Melissa, in 2009,

Alex was the best man.

Manny was also helped by Derek McGinnis, an above-the-knee amputee who met Manny's plane coming into San Antonio. Derek felt that it was his duty to welcome the new arrival because Manny and he were both in the Navy, and he kept a watchful eye over Manny throughout the recovery process. Derek told Manny about a group called the Sentinels of Freedom, headed by Mike Conklin, whose mission was to help veterans generate specific work opportunities. When Mike found out what kind of career Manny wanted to have, he connected Manny with the San Ramon Police Department, where he started behind the desk. While working, Manny attended and graduated from a law enforcement certificate program at Diablo Valley College, and he recently finished a four-year bachelor's degree in criminal justice from Grantham University. Manny is now in charge of entering people into local, national, and international criminal databases.

# *Wounded Warrior Amputee Softball Team*

Manny was one of the 20 originally selected players to come to camp in Tucson; however, his skills were not quite at the level to earn a spot on the initial traveling squad. Manny was grateful for the opportunity and appreciative of the softball paraphernalia that he was able to take home, and the team inspired him to improve his softball skills. So he joined a local team and started working to get better.

Manny also decided that he was going to stay in contact with the WWAST and improve to the point where he could get a new tryout for the traveling squad. He started training with Jon Stephens, a fellow police officer with a minor league background who graciously agreed to help Manny make the team. Jon had a batting cage at home, and he helped Manny learn how to leverage his body and prosthetic to turn on the ball. With

Jon's sons Austin and Braden shagging balls in the field, Manny worked tirelessly on fielding, throwing, and hitting mechanics. A year later, after finishing school, Manny returned to the WWAST as a regular.

Manny's life has been about taking challenging circumstances and turning them into rewarding second chances. Along the way he has been helped by caring teams of people who have selflessly given their time to help him improve, and he appreciates all of their efforts immensely. He is proud to have recovered to the point where he can work at the police station, enjoy time with his family, and contribute as a member of the WWAST. His wife, Melissa, whom he has known since sixth grade, pushes him to train hard and supports him while he is away on the road. As of this writing, they have a two-year-old son, Darren, and a two-month-old daughter, Alina.

Photo courtesy of Manny Del Rio

Photo courtesy of Manny Del Rio

Photo courtesy of Manny Del Rio

Photo courtesy of Manny Del Rio

Photo courtesy of Manny Del Rio

Photo courtesy of Lisa Macias

# AFTERWORD

## POST TRAUMATIC GROWTH

## AND DEVELOPMENT

## "LIFE WITHOUT A LIMB IS LIMITLESS"

The WWAST members profiled in this book came from every corner of the United States. Some grew up on a farm, some grew up in the inner city. Some players relied on stable families, others overcame instability. Some served in the Marines, others in the Army, and one served in the Navy. Each experienced a unique injury that resulted in a specific form of amputation, and each type of amputation required a different form of rehabilitation. On the surface, the backgrounds, life experiences, and injuries are completely unique, and it's tough to see what everyone has in common outside of an amazing story of recovery that ended with participation in the WWAST.

When you probe a little deeper, however, you see a pattern in the stories that shines through in the narrative of each player. It is a pattern that David Van Sleet recognized immediately, and it is part of the backbone of the WWAST. The elements are not easy to replicate, and many of them seem serendipitous at first. If you are looking to build an organization to help wounded veterans, however, you may find that the pieces that seem incidental are really part of a blueprint for a successful, caring, and effective organization.

The first element is starting with a core group of veterans that are determined to reclaim something that was temporarily taken away from them by a catastrophic injury. In the case of the WWAST, the players were seeking to regain their identity as athletes, so the initial motivation was regaining a competitive identity on an equal field of play where their opponents would have to take them seriously. But, as David is the first to admit, athletics is just one way to stimulate connection and rehabilitation. Every person has a unique personal, interpersonal, and social identity. As long as the identity is genuine, which athletics was for this team, it can serve as a powerful driver of healthy behavior.

The second element is an awareness that no one makes it back from the depths of a traumatic injury alone. As the stories in this book have demonstrated, caring behavior by outside parties is welcome at every stage of the process. For David and the WWAST, the decision was made to create a group at the post-recovery stage to help veterans build a bridge back to a healthy athletic identity. As you saw in the player narratives, however, people who connected with the players at every step of the process made an enormous difference. It is tough to imagine Bobby's path to recovery without Jack and Barbara, or Manny fulfilling his dream to join the police force without the Sentinels. Whether it was a veteran visiting the hospital, a community group lending support, or a family member putting their life on hold to aid in recovery, it is clear that caring action is helpful at every point it is offered.

The third element is an understanding that people thrive when they get a chance to be a part of something bigger than themselves. Most veterans are inspired by a genuine love of their country, their fellow servicemen and women, and the branch of the military they serve. When a solider is injured in combat, the first thing they lose is membership in a broad, supportive team with a unified purpose. At many levels, that is one of David's most important insights. He knew that the WWAST could become a new team for this group, and when the players had a new team they would have a new sense of purpose that would drive their recovery.

The last and most important element is giving veterans a chance to serve again. David's military background helped him understand from the beginning that injured soldiers do not want charity—they want a chance to serve their country in a capacity that makes a difference. When the WWAST takes the field, they give each player a chance to raise money for important charities, provide fans with a great show, and serve as an inspiration for people recovering from injuries. At its core, it is a service organization, and that is a perfect model for a group of soldiers who were willing to sacrifice everything for their country.

It is never easy, as David would be the first to tell you, and there are barriers at every stage of development. Even if you have a successful model, you may not just luck into leaders like Matt and Josh showing up for training camp. But there is an element beyond luck that helps explain why the WWAST has had the impact they have had. It is an organization that understands that caring, service, and team are the foundation of healthy rehabilitation. When those factors are combined with a group of veterans as special as the group profiled in this book, amazing things can happen.

*Matt, Nick & Josh at the USS Arizona Memorial –*
*Pearl Harbor, Honolulu, Hawaii*

# ACKNOWLEDGEMENTS

The prospect of entering the world of Wounded Warrior Amputee Softball Team players, their coaches, family, friends, benefactors, fans, and professional support groups was daunting. Would these people allow a stranger to come in their midst and ask questions about the most painful periods of their lives with honesty and civility? In fact, to a person, they were open, available, curious and helpful. Many tears and laughs were shared by both sides of the conversations. For people not experienced in being a part of getting the information for a book accurate and right, confirming these facts and events can be very tedious. Again, all respondents found ways to be helpful without any sense of being put-upon. For that they have my deepest appreciation.

David Van Sleet, originator and leader of the idea and the team that has sprung from it, was clear from the outset. All efforts would be handled with respect and regard for everyone involved, including the writing team. That relationship target was kept in sight from the first moment until now, and I expect it will last as David and the team continue to gain benefit from that core philosophy. Spend any personal and group time with the guys and those they care about and it is easy to feel a pervasive team spirit, along with consideration and interest in the welfare of others. There is no better atmosphere from which to gather difficult information.

I am particularly grateful to David and the nine players, Matt, Josh, Saul, Nick, Tim, Bobby, Nate, Spanky, and Manny, for allowing me to help them tell their stories in *Battlefield to Ball Field*. The level of cooperation was enormous from the perspectives of time and material, and each one had a way of helping the stranger feel welcomed and appreciated for putting in the effort required to create this book. They also allowed their significant others to participate to enrich the depth of the material and many expressed appreciation for the information gathering efforts on their behalf.

There is a poster at the beginning of the color section that says, "This Is Their Story." From the beginning of the project two years ago, including my first conversations with David Van Sleet, telling that story has been our mission. It could not have happened without everyone staying on that theme. We might have seemed a bit monotonous at times, but keeping a specific focus and tying that focus to a consistent process enabled the project to come to life.

The book proper does its best to describe the characteristics of the men who each earned a place on the team roster. Their character, resolve and commitment were instrumental in moving the book stages along, especially during difficult and painful memories. It should also be noted that family members both quoted and referenced for background accuracy gave of themselves to the level of personal pain when recounting those moments of uncertainty and anguish associated with the realities of terrible, life-threatening injuries sustained by sons and brothers thousands of miles away. They have been a constant motivation to make sure these pages bring support and help to others.

David and the team have many benefactors who were there in the early years and remain loyal to this day. Many of the people who had supporting roles during the pivotal year (November 2010–November 2011) have been mentioned in brief. Most were able to provide interview time to give us a wider sense of the story entirely through their personal generosity of spirit. There are many people who were interviewed who are not specifically mentioned in the book. You have our most sincere thanks.

In order to gain a lot of information in a short time about issues associated with the problems encountered by team members and their loved ones, I was helped by a number of experts in this field who gave time willingly and effectively. An incomplete list of those whose efforts stood out are David Van Sleet, Billie J. Randolph, Katy Hoeft, Jessica Grede, and Derek McGinnis, who contributed to my understanding of the positive potential available after trauma.

The Clear Vision Publishing team assembled for this project were dedicated and tireless. As always, Bill Miller set the tone for consistent movement towards seemingly impossible goals. Whenever the inevitable snag occurred, Bill found ways to get the wheels back on the tracks without drawing any attention to himself. His steadfast belief in the goals and objectives of *Battlefield to Ball Field* never wavered.

My sons, Joe Dougherty and David Clarfield, contributed substantially to every aspect of the writing, including editing final drafts. Joseph's keen awareness of the core values of the work have been present in both *Best of the Best* and *Battlefield to Ball Field*. He has a way of maintaining a steady course through complex ideas that never ceases to amaze. David has a precise and sensitive ear that lends depth and rhythm to his edited works. He is also a veteran of other CV Publishing projects, where his contributions are sought after within the organization.

Danielle Camarco came to the project at the eleventh hour and transcribed over 100 hours of recorded interviews into well-organized research material. She also sorted electronic communication with grace and a smoothness usually only seen in someone well beyond her years. Whenever there was a need to move from interview to final research document, she had a ready smile while showing an effortlessly effective array of solutions.

In San Antonio, Texas, Larry and Kathryn Lackmann found a number of ingenius and caring ways to help us during our stay. Their efforts are much appreciated.

My sister, Robin Tolvin, on a number of occasions augmented her schedule to find ways to be directly helpful and supportive to her brother. Her keen insights and attention to detail are an always welcome addition to any program or project I have undertaken over the years. I rely on her counsel for too many things to detail and appreciate her candor and strength of purpose as a lifelong given.

My daughter Sarah took time out to accompany her dad as photographer for a grueling weekend excursion to game sites in Florida. Her pictures and her enthusiasm for the project are much appreciated.

Jim Knipper added his typical levels of support to the CV Publishing effort by assuring that there would be a fulfillment structure once the book reached its publication date. His staff of effective specialists, particularly Amy Luongo, can always be counted on to assist customers while making new friends in the process.

Mike Krupa has been with Clear Vision since our 2004 rebirth, and never ceases to help and inform. No matter what the challenge, he has a storehouse of creative solutions to bring to any publication problem. And he is without peer in matching an effervescent mood with an ability to respond tirelessly to marathon responsibilities.

Book projects take time away from other family functions and the burden to keep us going on all cylinders falls to my wife of 29 years, Patricia. Without her ceaseless attention to crucial family matters, there could be no projects, good or otherwise. *My debt to her is beyond words.*

# Wounded Warrior
# Amputee Softball Team

## OUR MISSION

The mission of the Wounded Warrior Amputee Softball Team (WWAST) is to raise awareness, through exhibition and celebrity softball games, of the sacrifices and resilience of our military, and to highlight their ability to rise above any challenge. Our goal is to show other amputees and the general population that these athletes, through extensive rehabilitation and training, are able to live out their desires and play the sport they loved.

## OUR TEAM

The WWAST is comprised of young, competitive, athletic veterans and active duty soldiers who have lost limbs while serving their country in the military after 9/11. The team includes individuals with a variety of amputations of the arm, leg, and foot. Some are still in the service, others are attending college thanks to the Post-9/11 GI Bill, while still others have moved on to new careers.

## OUR VISION

WWAST athletes are amputees who continue to push the limits of modern prosthetic technology as it allows more and more applications. Of course, our dream would be the return of our soldiers from harm's way without the resulting loss of life and limb. Until such a time, our vision is to support and honor our soldiers' and veterans' sacrifices, and to show other amputees and everyone who sees or hears about us that life without a limb is limitless.

WOUNDED WARRIOR

AMPUTEE SOFTBALL TEAM, INC.

A PUBLIC CHARITY UNDER

SECTION 501(c)(3),

INTERNAL REVENUE CODE

CONTRIBUTIONS ARE TAX DEDUCTIBLE

*I want to take this opportunity to thank the many individuals and organizations that helped and benefited the Wounded Warrior Amputee Softball Team during the early years in countless ways, for without them we would not be the strong and thriving organzation that we have become — and please forgive me if my memory has failed and I have neglected to include your name below.*

**– David Van Sleet**

## *Special Thanks to the Following Individuals and Organizations*

Annie Izquierdo

Kelly Brooks

Carston Foy

Javeriah Haleem

Brian Venerick

Jon Gardner

Susan Bowers

Fred Downs

Michelle Izquierdo-Phelps

Melissa Stockwell

Sally Compton

Laura Levering

Dave Davis

Tucson, AZ VA Medical Center

Larry Brushett

Jeff Miller

Roger Hockey

Richard Sanders

Tom Siter

Doug Barnette

Jason Dunavan

Lara Potter

Nicole Murray

Jay Marsh

Joe Verbanic

George Mason University

Bill Haden

Steve Scott

Roy Lawson

Ryan Coe

Del Pickney

Tom Calicott

Dave Stewart

Al Miotke

Ed Eggly

Alex Galiana

Ryan Kules

John Loosen

American Legion Post 177

Pam Pelano

Jerry Pelano

Tamara Baldanza

Margaritaville
     Hospitality Group

Brian Drummond
Dianne Janczewski
Stacy Natoli
Jason Billingsley
Susan Rodio
Tom Plant
Wynn Las Vegas
Mason Inn
Tucson Marriott
    University Park
Laura Gipe
The Galt House
The Seelbach Hilton Hotel
Tinker Air Force Base
Danville, IL Police Department
Danville, IL Fire Department
Sue Carney
American Postal Workers Union
Highland Woods Golf &
    Country Club
HBO Real Sports
    with Bryant Gumbel
Sports Illustrated Magazine
Phil Taylor
ESPN
Maury Nieber
Jahn Tihansky
US Naval Academy
Walter Reed National
    Military Medical Center
University of Arizona Women's
Softball Team
George Mason University
    Women's Softball Team
Brion's Grille
Charlie Crone
James Moeller
Greg Mahoney

John Glufling
Christina Billingslley
Michelle Shumway
Alex Shumway
Dave Shumway
Laurie Hickey
Avi Spector
Trevor LeMaster
Victoria Ross
Military Order of The Purple
    Heart Service Foundation
Sandy Silva
Tempe Mission Palms Hotel
Dennis Turner
Midori Johnson
Phiten
Rick Jackson
Boombah
Kyle McGowan
Dave Aichinger
New Era
Majestic
Washington Nationals
Scott Creagan
Jordan Traynor
Graphic Connection
Kevin Reynolds
Emily Moak
USA Men's National Slow
    Pitch Team
Israel Negron
John Lytle
Kim Pinegar
Tamara Pinegar
Amy Hoeft
Össur
Matt Ballantine
Dave McGill

John Hillerich

Wendy Baur

Rocky Bleier

InDyne

Don Bishop

Janis Bishop

Jeffrey Reimer

Knight Point Systems

Bob Eisiminger

Buddy Biancalana

Brad Borowy

Kyle Bostwick

Dana Bowman

Cindy Brannon

Brittany Brannon

Diane Briskey

Mike Britt

Nate Bry

Custom Apparel

Kurt Busch

American Forces Foundation

Patricia Driscoll

Jose Cardenal

Judy Williams

Louisville, KY VA
        Medical Center

Lori Wilkinson

American Legion Riders

Kevin Mench

Jack Van Sleet

Polly Van Sleet

Christine Tanavusa

University of Alabama
        Women's Softball Team

Samantha Corlew

Billie Jane Randolph

Jody Boone

McKenzie Boone

Madison Boone

Dan Kaseman

Barry Hickey

Jim Rodio

Hayley O'Mara

Patriot Riders

Curtis Pride

Gallaudet University

Carolyn Clinton

Brian Kittle

Mahesh Mansukhani

Mark Lerner

Marla Lerner Tanenbaum

Allen Hermeling

Joanna Comfort

Alexandra Schauffler

Brian Beck

Kim Billingsley

Jola Janczewski

Rick Redman

Robbie Robinson

Gary LaFon

Stan Finch

Katy Hoeft

Donna Reimer

Karen Klasi

Rich Hoppe

Charlie Dobbins

Regensis Biomedical

Tom Eisiminger

USSSA

Baden

Rusty Trudeau

Mitzi Hodges

Summer Robbins

Jeff Jackson

Jim Click

Jon Pizzagalli